The Ultimate Beginners Guide for App Programming and Development Made Easy

by Neo Monefa

Table of Contents

1. Introduction
2. App Platforms
3. History of Mobile Apps
4. App Catagories
5. Different Types of Mobile Apps
6. Paid vs. Free Apps
7. Tips on Choosing App Type and Content
8. Getting Started – App Development Basics
9. Where to Find Developers
10. Common Mistakes to Avoid When Outsourcing

11. DIY Basic Development
12. App Testing
13. Submitting and Publishing Your App
14. App Maintenance
15. App Marketing
16. App Monetization
17. Tying Loose Ends
18. Conclusion
19. THANK YOU FOR READING!

1. Introduction

The next time you are having lunch at your favorite restaurant, pay attention to the people around you. Most likely, more than half of the people in the restaurant have their eyes glued to their mobile phones or tablets. In the Unites States alone, it is estimated that over 91 million people own and use smartphones. Worldwide, over one billion smartphones are currently in use. In fact, you are probably one of the millions of people who own a smartphone and I am sure you know exactly what an app is and just how essential it is in having a complete and enjoyable smartphone experience.

Though, I must admit, I was never an I.T. guy and do not have any programming knowledge at all. In fact, the only reason I got into mobile apps development business is because of my dear friend, Spark So. He is always fascinated by the concept of earning income in autopilot mode via outsourcing. Then one day he told me he has quit his boring banking job at one of the top European banks and was preparing to launch his first app. Though I did not really pay much attention at that time. But six months later, he told me he was earning consistently around $15,000 USD per month – and as of this writing, he's making around $30,000 USD a month! I was both shocked and surprised because I never would have thought that an app that cost only $0.99 USD would allow him to earn such a substantial and steady income – far higher than his banking earnings. Throughout out my life, I was taught that the only way to achieve stable income growth was through employment in big multinational corporations.

The truth is, anyone can do this too, regardless of his academic or work experiences. All you need is a computer, mobile phone and an Internet connection to communicate with freelancers that build the apps for you. Yes, that's right, you don't need to know any programming languages or be an expert in graphic design! It's actually quite embarrassing to say but I still don't know how to submit or update my apps, I simply outsource all the work to my freelance developers.

This industry allows you to work anywhere, anytime, and in many ways exciting than you think. You are essentially selling virtual goods that need minimum maintenance while earning real cash. Obviously, there's more to just writing up a job description for your developers. That's essentially why I have compiled this e-book to help anyone interested in becoming an apps entrepreneur and start tapping into this ever-growing industry. So, if you are interested in living a stress-free life and determined to build your own apps portfolio, simply read through and let me guide you all the way to your dream business.

2. App Platforms

Before jumping into the deep end of the mobile app development pool, let us first explore the basics about apps and the app industry. In this chapter, you'll discover just how apps have evolved from preinstalled productivity tools on handheld PDAs to sophisticated programs with a wide variety of functionalities.

But first, let's look at the different app platforms that are currently in use in millions of smartphones worldwide.

Different App Platforms

Not all smartphones are created equal and the differences between the types of smartphones aren't only skin deep. Beyond its physical form, smartphones can also differ in operating systems (OS) or platforms. In this section, we'll look at the different platforms that run smartphone apps.

1. iOS

The iOS is the platform distributed by Apple for iPhones, iPads and iPod Touch devices. The apps are downloaded from the App Store and are installed on the device either through syncing the unit to iTunes on a computer or laptop or from the unit itself.

Advantages

•   Because the iOS was the first operating system to introduce an app store, it has more apps available for download than the other platforms.

•   In line with the previous point, most apps on the app store are exclusive for the iOS only. This means that iOS users have a big advantage with the choices of premium and high-quality apps that it can download. A lot of developers also use the iOS as a testing platform and would release their apps for the iOS first before creating a version for the other platforms.

• The most recent version of iOS made social networking integration easier for its users. You can now upload photos directly and automatically to Facebook, Twitter and other social media sites after syncing your accounts on your device.

• Since the very first version of the iOS, very little has changed in terms of its user interface. Because of this, the consistency of the user's general smartphone experience is preserved. For example, an iPhone user who upgrades from the iPhone 3G to the iPhone 5 won't have much trouble using the device since its general functionality is similar for both versions.

Disadvantages

• The most recent iOS update has removed the YouTube and Google Maps apps, leaving less than satisfactory replacements that have caused a bit of PR foibles for Apple.

• While battery life is more of a hardware issue, it should also be noted that a short battery life also directly affects the users' ability to access and use apps, especially the apps that require Internet connection or GPS tracking.

2. Android

This platform is Linux-based and owned by Google. Unlike the iOS, Android is opensourced which allows developers, wireless carriers and manufacturers to modify and distribute apps for Android smartphones. Android is designed to run on smartphones and tablets that are primarily designed as touchscreen devices. Android apps can be purchased and downloaded from Google Play – the app store of the platform.

Advantages

• Android users can also enjoy using other Google products and services such as YouTube and Google Maps without having to download these apps separately.

• Android gives users more options when it comes to app sharing. For example, a note that you have created using Google Keep can be shared via Bluetooth, to your Facebook wall, messaging, e-mail, Viber, Dropbox and other apps on your device that will allow it.

• Unlike with iOS which allows the usage of only one iTunes account at any given time, Android lets its users sync multiple Gmail accounts and keep them all logged in simultaneously.

• Personalization is possible with Android because of its open-source nature. Developers can personalize how the OS works on their device and improve the existing software structures that Google and the phone manufacturers have done.

Flash video support which allows users to watch videos or play games from their browser.

• Android has fewer restrictions when it comes to the apps that it publishes on Google Play, making it easier for developers to publish their apps for downloads.

Disadvantages

• The Android OS is a multi-tasking system and though it might be useful for active phone users, it takes up a lot of your phone's read access memory (RAM) and battery because a lot of these apps continue to run in the background even after closing the app.

• Not all Android phones have the same features. Unlike with the iOS where its interface is pretty much similar across all phone versions, Android phones vary greatly depending on its manufacturer. For example, an HTC Droid DNA and a Samsung

Galaxy Note II will function, feel and perform differently despite both using the Android Jelly Bean 4.1 version.

• App compatibility can become an issue because of the wide variety of processors that run Android. Because Android phones are made by different manufacturers, an app may not be compatible to all of them. This is especially problematic for game developers who may not be able to release universal versions of their game that is guaranteed to run no matter what the device's processor is.

3. BlackBerry

This platform is used on Research In Motion (RIM) devices and is considered as one of the earliest platforms for smartphones. It is typically the platform of choice for individuals who rely heavily on their gadgets for work-related tasks such as accessing and responding to e-mails and viewing documents, spreadsheets and power point presentations. Apps are available for purchase and download at the BlackBerry App World.

Advantages

• Probably the two main reasons why people opt for BlackBerry phones are its email integration and peer-to-peer messaging or the BlackBerry Messenger (BBM). Users can easily receive and send e-mails as they would text messages. The BBM is also very useful for communicating with other BlackBerry users all over the world.

• Like with Android phones, BlackBerry phones have expandable memory which allows the user to download more apps or to save more files to an external memory card.

BlackBerry uses a military-grade security platform to protect its users' personal data.

• BlackBerry phones can be synced to different computers simultaneously. This feature is especially helpful if you want to update schedules or address books in multiple computers.

Disadvantages

•   Most BlackBerry phones have QWERTY keyboards and it wasn't until recently that RIM launched a touch screen phone. Avid mobile gamers and smartphone purists find it hard to overlook BlackBerry's hardware and design deficiencies.

•   Web browsing on a BlackBerry phone leaves much to be desired. Users have to wait considerably longer for images and videos to load when browsing the Internet.

•   Even if the BlackBerry App World was one of the first app stores launched, it still has a very limited number of apps available for download. The BlackBerry user interface (UI) also limits the types of apps that the devices can use.

4. Windows

The Windows operating system is no longer exclusively for personal computers and laptops. The company has released a mobile version that runs on smartphones manufactured by HTC, Samsung, Nokia and Asus. The OS boasts of live tiles that make app navigation a breeze. Users can also create and access office documents and emails on the go. Over 130,000 apps can be purchased and downloaded from the Windows Phone Store.

Advantages

•   Even if Windows is designed with the corporate market in mind, it doesn't alienate its younger market. The Windows Phone Store has a wide variety of apps that aren't limited to only business and productivity uses.

•   Cloud computing makes it possible for users to sync MSOffice documents, emails and other Microsoft programs that are typically used in an office setting.

- If you're generally familiar with the Microsoft environment, you'll find it easy to navigate through a Windows Mobile OS.

Disadvantages

- Windows phones do not support Flash or even Silverlight videos on its browsers.

The volume and variety of apps is limited compared to the iOS or Android. Though this may change in the near future as more manufacturers produce more Windows phones.

- The UI can be complicated for those who are not familiar with the Windows environment.

Not all app developers are well-versed in creating cross-platform apps that are readily available for all operating systems. The limitations in phone features and designs also make it difficult, if not impossible for developers to release uniformed versions that would consistently function for all types of platforms.

Another consideration would be the OS versions. Apple, Google, BlackBerry and Windows make it a point to upgrade their OS to allow for more advanced functionalities. To address this, developers also upgrade their apps to match the platforms' newest versions.

3. History of Mobile Apps

Believe it or not, Apple is not the first company to create and launch a smartphone. In 1994, IBM introduced Simon to the world – the first mobile phone that integrates telephone and personal digital assistant (PDA) features in a single device.

Despite only having a 1 MB memory and storage capacity, Simon came with a calendar, appointment scheduler, handwritten notepad capability and a world clock. Users can upgrade their units to allow third-party programs (now more popularly known as apps) to be installed and used.

The next big smartphone to hit the market was the Nokia 9000 which used the GEOS V3.0 operating system. This smartphone was launched in 1996. Its notable apps included a web browser, smart messaging and digital camera connectivity feature.

For the next few years, phone manufacturers launched several devices that were marketed as PDA handhelds. These models had limited telephone features and were more focused on making it easier for users to schedule appointments, access e-mails and keep track of events through calendars. The three dominating operating systems (OS) during this period were Palm OS, BlackBerry OS and Windows CE.

The earliest PDA versions already had apps pre-installed and needed upgrading and external installations to add more apps. It wasn't uncommon during the late 1990's to early 2000's for professionals to carry two devices – a mobile phone and a PDA.

It wasn't until 2002 when Research In Motion (RIM) launched the BlackBerry 5810 – a handheld PDA with communication capabilities. The apps that are pre-installed on the device are what you would typically expect on a PDA – calendar, appointment scheduler, e-mail and Internet connectivity. In order to install new apps, users had to download third-party applications on their computers and then sync the device using a cable to transfer and install the app to the phone.

RIM had very little competition when it came to smartphones. There were manufacturers like Samsung and Nokia that released phones with Internet connectivity and basic apps but the design and phone features still fell short.

In 2007 however, the smartphone industry was forever changed when Apple launched the very first iPhone. Apple combined the touch screen, multi-tasking environment of its top-selling iPod Touch with telephony functionalities to create a powerful smartphone. The device came with a limited number of apps, including Apple's iTunes which allowed the device to double as a music player.

The Apple App Store was launched a year later on July with only 500 available apps for download. In its first weekend, Apple reported that it has reached a milestone of 10 million downloads. By November, the available apps for download swelled to 10,000 and by early 2009, over 500 million apps have been downloaded from the Apple App Store.

Google entered the mobile phone operating system in the same year that the first iPhone was launched. Android-operated phones were manufactured by manufacturers such as Samsung, Motorola and HTC. The Android Market was launched in October of 2008 with only 50 apps available for download. By March of 2009, Android offered 2,300 apps with paid applications also available for its users.

Not to be outdone, the BlackBerry App World was formally launched in 2009 which allowed BlackBerry users to purchase, download and install apps on the device itself. RIM reported reaching up to 10 million app downloads per day. The App World featured apps developed by BlackBerry, as well as those created by third-party developers.

Another mobile app store that was launched in 2009 was Nokia's Ovi Store. Upon launching, over 1,000 apps were available for download although 90% of these were paid apps.

By the end of 2009, the Apple App Store was the leading app market place in terms of app submissions, sales and downloads. The company announced that they have reached the three billionth download milestone at the end of that year. The Android Market had about 20,000 apps, over half of which were free to download and use. The Ovi Store was also successful that year with up to one million downloads per day.

The following year was a big year for the app industry. BlackBerry reached the milestone of 1.5 million downloads per day, as well as launching BlackBerry App World, Android reached its one billionth download while Apple reached its three billionth download. The Windows Phone Marketplace was also introduced in 2010 along with its Windows 7 smartphones

This was also the year that the first iPad was released by Apple which sparked a demand for tablet personal computers (PC). Though technically, Android tablets were being sold in the market before the iPads were introduced, Apple dominated the tablet market due to the success of its iPhones.

The high wave of mobile apps continued on to 2011 as smartphones become more prevalent in society across different age groups. Apple had approved its 500 thousandth app, BlackBerry had three million downloads per day, the Ovi Store had six million downloads per day with over 80,000 available apps and the Windows Marketplace had 30,000 apps available.

By 2012, Nokia's Ovi Store was discontinued along with the Symbian OS that the manufacturer has been using for its smartphones. Nokia now uses the Windows Mobile OS for its newer models.

In the same year, the Android Marketplace became known as Google Play and its features were not just app-centered. Android users can also use the Play Store to download music, e-books, videos and other media compatible with their devices.

In the next section, we'll look at the current market positions of the existing app platforms and their app stores. We'll also look at the different demographics of app users so that you can get a better idea of who uses what types of apps.

4. App Catagories

Before getting started on building your app, it helps to know what kind of animal you are dealing with.

App Categories

It's important for you to know the different app categories for different OS and platforms for you to be able to thoughtfully scout out your competition.

Let's first look at the categories for the Apple App Store:

Apple App Store

Books

In this category, you'll find electronic versions of books, comics and mangas, as well as different types of readers for those materials. There are also literature-centered social networking apps that let users share their favorite titles and what they're reading at the moment.

Business

This is generally where business utilities and tools go to though you may find some quirky apps every now and then.

Catalogs

Brands, retail stores, tattoo artists and interior decorators are some examples of the types of businesses that use this category. If you are looking to showcase products or even just producing your own smiley, this is a good place to get your app noticed.

Education

The apps here have one goal: to teach or educate users about specific topics. *Face-value*

Entertainment

Entertainment apps are all about the user's enjoyment. Novelty apps go here, as well as memes and fun simulators.

Finance

This category is for apps that help in money management, keeping track of the stock market and the financial sector in general.

Food & Drink

As the title implies, this category feature recipes, wine tasting notebooks, restaurant ratings and a lot more.

Games

This is the most popular app category and as you can imagine, there is a lot of competition for the #1 spot. It is also one of the few categories that have made first-time developers into successful entrepreneurs. *Bubble Popper*
Drinking Game — by college

Health & Fitness

This is the category for apps that help improve one's health and fitness level.

Lifestyle

This is a broad category that can include apps for gardening, phone personalization, parenting, arts and crafts and scrapbooking.

Medical

This is the category for medical professionals like doctors and nurses. This is also where First Aid and pregnancy apps go.

Music

Category for apps that stream, play, modifies or identifies music. It can also contain apps about the music industry, bands and artists.

Navigation

Any app that helps people locate places go here.

News

For apps that update users of the latest happenings.

Newsstand

For apps that require subscriptions for content. These publications can be accessed from its dedicated icon or through the App Store. Examples of Newsstand apps are the New York Times and Vogue Magazine.

Photo & Video

For apps that lets users take, edit, modify, document and share photos and videos.

Productivity

Apps that make users' lives easier to manage. Popular apps are to-do lists, note takers and grocery lists.

Reference

Reference guides for any topic goes here. Could be anything from textbooks, dictionaries to bartending menus.

Social Networking

A category for apps that are extensions of social networking sites or helps in improving communications between users.

Sports

For anything sports-related like live scoring, game streaming and team updates. *Sports Rules for beginners*

Travel

For anything related to traveling like flight updates, hotel and restaurant finders, basic translations for phrases and currency converters.

Utilities

Apps in this category help in making life easier or make your phone operate better.

Weather

This is pretty self-explanatory. Anything to do with weather.

Let's now look at the sales statistics for different categories:

• The Games category has the largest share of available apps with 16.77%. Education and Entertainment come in second third with 11% and 9% respectively .
• Half of all available apps in the App Store are free. Only 20% of all apps are $0.99 and less than 1% is over $20 .
• There are over 600,000 iPhone/iPod Touch apps and over 300,000 iPad apps.

Android's Google Play

Books & Reference

Users can find book readers, textbooks, dictionaries and other reading materials.

Business

Apps that help users manage office needs like document readers, scanners, publishing, e-mail management. Also includes app that help in searching for jobs and projects.

Comics

This category is especially for comic book fans, creators and enthusiasts. Here you can find webcomics, comic readers and Internet meme generators, among others.

Communication

Apps that improve communication between users go here. Can include address book tools, instant messengers, dialers, web browsers and VOIP tools.

Education

A category for learning tools, study aids, review materials, educational games and the like.

Entertainment

From pranks to sound effects and movie streaming - anything and everything meant to entertain users can be found here.

Finance

The category for banking apps, payment portals, stock and market monitoring and other financial tools.

Health & Fitness

The category for diet monitoring, eating habits, exercise tools, health tips, calorie trackers and the like.

Libraries & Demo

This category is for developers who are looking for demo versions of software and tools.

Lifestyle

Apps that help improve a user's way of living go here. Includes alarm clocks, recipe books, bar lists and a slew of others.

Live Wallpaper

Apps and other materials that improve the visual aspect and GUI of the device go here.

Media & Video

Contains movie subscriptions, media remote controls, video downloads and streaming video apps.

Medical

For medically-related content and apps. Includes medical references, first aid manuals, study guide and calendars.

Music & Audio

Contains apps for music downloads, music streaming, audio books and other tools to make audio listening easier.

News & Magazines

For users who need to stay on top of what's happing, locally, nationwide or worldwide, they can find apps in this category to keep them updated.

Personalization

Apps and content to make phones visually prettier and more unique.

Photography

Apps in this category are all about photos and images – editing, sharing, taking, modifying, etc.

Productivity

Contains app that makes users' lives easier like to-do lists, reminders, alarms, etc.

Shopping

For coupons, sale announcements and online shopping apps, this is the category to go to.

Social

The category for social networking sites, GPS check-ins and information sharing.

Sports

Pretty self-explanatory. Anything sports-related goes here.

Tools

Apps that help users improve their devices' functionalities.

Travel & Local

Apps to make traveling and wandering easier.

Weather

Again, this category is pretty self-explanatory. Anything weather-related goes here.

Here are some Google Play stats for you to munch on:

- There are over 500,000 apps on Google Play. Over 50% are free apps.
- Entertainment apps are the most downloaded apps on Google Play. Personalization and Books & References is the second and third most downloaded respectively.
- Brain and Puzzle games are the most downloaded on Google Play .

5. Different Types of Mobile Apps

Native Apps

Native applications are designed and developed for a specific platform. From the planning to the production stage, a platform is already selected. This enables the developer to use specific tools and languages that are native to that specific OS. Native apps can also function without Internet or mobile connectivity.

Native apps are installed directly to the device. These are the apps that you will find on the different app stores of each platform. The versions of these apps vary depending on the OS of the device.

For example, the game Temple Run was first introduced to iOS devices before Android phones. If the developers submitted the exact same app to Android so that the game will be launched on both platforms simultaneously, the app might not work for Android users at all because not all programming language that runs on iOS is compatible with Android.

Here's a short summary of the different platform languages:

- Java for Android and BlackBerry
- Objective-C for iOS
- Visual C++ for Windows Mobile

Standardized development kits (SDKs) are typically provided by the platform companies. The SDKs are development tools and interface elements that a developer may include in the app like input fields or buttons.

As a first time developer, creating a native app can be a big challenge, especially if you're planning to have a version of your app for multiple platforms. If you are able to adjust and adapt to different languages however, the rewards are well worth the effort.

Native apps also have lots of benefits in terms of the quality and functionality of the app:

- **Multi-touch** features are only possible on native apps. These are touch screen gestures like pinch-spreads, double taps, swipes and other gestures that are completed using the UI.

- If your app heavily relies on the quality of the movements of your characters or material, a native app is the only type that will give you the fastest **graphics application programming interface (API).**

An API is essentially a programming protocol that enables different components of the program to communicate with each other. It is a library that contains a wide variety of actions which determine how the app will act while being used.

With a native app, APIs that deal with graphics and visuals will be much faster than on any other type of mobile apps. This is especially important if you are developing a game, a location-based app that uses GPS technology or an app that needs access to other components of the device like the clock or address book for example.

- If you're planning to develop an app that is heavy on the visuals and animation, a native app is better in providing **fluid animation** than other types of apps. Game, photo modification and video playing/streaming apps need the best quality of animation possible and native programming and development is necessary to make the app the highest quality it can be.

- Because people are already familiar with the different functionalities of their devices, native apps will give its users a relative **ease of use.**

So how are native apps designed and developed?

Native apps are programmed using an integrated development environment or IDE. Different platforms have different types of IDE. These IDEs contain platform-specific tools and materials required to make the app function the way you want it to function.

The downside of native apps is that it is more difficult to develop and it takes more time to go from the coding stage to the publishing phase. Native app developers are considered as some of the most sought-after mobile app programmers in the industry and for good reason.

If you're envisioning a simple native app with basic functionalities, you also have the option of using online app builders.

Using online app builders can save you money if you're planning to publish a simple app with basic functionalities. However, bear in mind that an app that has more specialized features will need more complicate programming, something that an online builder may not be able to provide for.

Mobile Web Apps

"HTML" may be a familiar set of letters to you if you have a background in developing web pages. HTML5 is a programming style for website pages that can also be used for mobile app development. You can also use CSS, JavaScript or a combination of the three styles.

These apps do not need to be installed on the device. The content of the app will be accessed using the device's browser so the quality of the app is largely dependent on the quality of the browser.

Developing mobile web apps are a lot easier compared with native apps. Maintenance for these types of apps is also compared to the others. Another advantage is that you can develop a single version of a mobile web app and it can be distributed to multiple platforms.

There is a wide variety of plugins and additional tools that can be added on an HTML source. This can help improve the users' experience when accessing the web page using different browsers or add additional features that can make your app look and feel like more than just another web page.

While many first-time developers consider creating mobile web apps for their first experimental project, there are some limitations that need to be considered:

•	There is **no multi-touch recognition.** The app will not be able to determine or recognize if two fingers are being used on the screen, it is the browser that will react with multi-touch gestures. Because different users use different browsers, the actions that multi-touch gestures create vary greatly.

•	As in websites and web pages, users will not be able to access your app's contents without an Internet connection which will make **offline accessibility** impossible. If you want your users to be able to access your app's content with or without Internet, you may need to consider developing other app types.

•	Because mobile apps are completely dependent on the devices' browsers and the websites' servers, **quality-control for the app is extremely difficult.** Even if you put in your best efforts to create a visually appealing and fully functional app, if the device's browser out-of-date or the site's server is down, the user will not be able to get the most out of your app.

Mobile apps are developed using HTML5, CSS3, JavaScript along with frameworks such as PHP or Python. There are plenty of web-based tools that you can use to create mobile apps which you will learn all about in a later chapter.

Though features and functionalities may be limited, mobile apps are excellent springboards for mobile app beginners. Developing these types of apps can help you gain a better understanding of the app industry in general.

Client-Server and Hybrid Apps

These apps have similarities with native apps in the sense that it has to be installed on the device and that it needs access to some of the device's functionalities such as the camera or address book, for example. The main difference between client-server and native apps is that the former needs to have Internet in order to work.

Banking and online shopping apps are some examples for these types of app. Without an Internet connection, you will still be able to see the basic interface of the app but you won't be able to access the content of the apps since it has to be downloaded from a separate server. Another example would be social networking apps like Facebook and Twitter. Before you can access your account's content, you need to have an Internet connection.

Hybrid apps on the other hand can still work without Internet connection but to unlock additional features or functionalities, you'll need Internet connectivity. For example, mobile games can still be played even without having to connect to the Internet but you won't be able to play with other players, make in-game purchases or post scores on a leader board.

In the development side, hybrid and client-server apps are written in web languages such as HTML5, CSS3 or JavaScript – like mobile web apps but unlike web apps, hybrid apps are wrapped in native code (Objective-C for the iPhone, Java for Android, etc.).

These types of apps be developed at a moderate speed and is fairly easy to maintain. It combines the advantages of native apps like access to device features and better graphics with the advantages of mobile apps, notably the development time. Here are other advantages:

- Because it takes less time to develop, it is more cost-effective than native apps but its quality in terms of graphics and features is not sacrificed.

- It is easier to modify the app programming to make it compatible with other platforms. Remember that only the wrapper of the code is written in a native app language so it won't require as much modification as native app. Web-based languages are universally recognized by different platforms so edits for this part of the programming are minimal.

- Majority of app users won't be able to tell the difference between native and hybrid apps, especially for apps that are not greatly interactive. This is great news for developers who are planning to create simple apps that only require moderate internet connectivity, push notifications and other basic phone features. Best of all, the app will not be launched on a browser.

While native apps are still considered as the most ideal type of app for income generation, hybrids and client-server apps are quickly becoming more popular in the app development industry. More individuals and small businesses are realizing its resource-saving potential without having to cross out vital features that make an app unique and valuable.

However, you also need to bear in mind that while the advantages of both native and mobile apps are present in hybrid apps, so do some the disadvantages of both types. For one, hybrid apps are noticeably slower than native apps in terms of performance. Because the bulk of hybrid app codes are still written in web languages, it is still bound by its limitations even if it is combined with native app programming.

Another drawback is its emulated look and feel compared to native apps. It may appear like a native app on the surface and it may have native capabilities but it still would not look and feel exactly like a native app. If you're planning to build an app that is heavily reliant on a device's tools and functionalities, you may need to opt to have the bulk of your coding in native languages.

Native, mobile web and hybrid apps have become increasingly essential in making a smartphone more valuable, enjoyable and functional to a user. Statistics also show more people are now switching their outdated mobile phones for more modern smartphones and they aren't hesitating to store their credit card information with app stores for easy purchases.

With a good idea of what type of app you can use for your first app, let's now look the considerations that you need to make when choosing between publishing a free, "freemium" or paid app.

6. Paid vs. Free Apps

Aside from choosing the type of app to develop, you will also need to decide whether to make your app free for download or if you will charge users for a copy. There has been much debate about this issue for years and it all boils down to one question: what is your objective with your app?

Take a look at these considerations that you need to review when deciding whether to release a paid or free app:

- **How your app functions.** If you're planning to launch a simple mobile app that only brings users to a specific web page, chances are that people won't be willing to pay for something that they can do themselves, app or no app. On the other hand, if your app has a wide variety of functionalities, people will be more inclined to purchase it.

- **Your app's content.** Apps that have a large volume of convenient and exclusive content sell well on app stores because it's something that people will be looking for. Examples are recipe books, e-books and manuals. If your app has limited content,

- **In-app purchases.** If you're developing a gaming app, you should consider whether you want to feature additional in-game items that users can purchase. Many game developers have released free versions of comprehensive games but have made up in profit through in-app purchases.

- **In-app advertising.** It's a typical practice in the app industry to offer paid ad-free versions of apps while the free ones have advertisements. Many developers actually report that they have made more money through in-app advertising than in paid downloads.

Check out any app store and you'll see that apps can either be paid or free and there are certain apps that have both free and paid versions. Let's look at advantages and disadvantages of both focusing on free apps first.

Advantages of Free Apps

A lot of people believe that paid apps are better than free apps in terms of overall quality. This misconception has been disproven time and again as hundreds of developers publish highly rated apps on every category across different platforms. Take Candy Crush Saga, for example. This app is downloaded and played by millions of smartphone and tablet users from all over the world yet it is a "freemium" app.

There are plenty of good reasons why developers and app publishers release their products without asking for an outright payment from their customers. Here are some of the most essential ones:

- **"Payouts ain't easy."** Platforms usually take a cut out of app sales. For example, Apple takes 30% of the price of an app for every purchase. So if you sold your app at the App Store at $0.99 per download, $0.30 goes to Apple and $0.70 goes to you. This may not seem like a lot but if you sell 10,000 copies of your app, instead of getting $9,900, you'll only end up getting $6,930 after Apple takes its cut.

Besides the cut that platforms get from app sales, there's also the issue of timely payments. Unfortunately, you won't get your cut of your app sales immediately after the purchase has been completed. Google Play, for example releases pay outs a few days after the end of each month. Other app stores are not as quick as Google Play when it comes to payouts and waiting time can reach weeks after each month.

Another challenge is informally called the "sales threshold". This basically means that unless you have reached a sales or payout quota, the app store won't release a payment for the app sales you've had so far. Some app stores require as much as $250 minimum in app sales before they release any form of payment. With free apps, you won't be at the mercy of app stores to get your portion.

- **Freedom in advertising.** A lot of app users opt for paid versions because of the absence of advertising. In this case, developers will have to rely on strong sales in order to profit from their products – something that isn't always guaranteed. Free apps with no paid versions almost solely rely on advertising income to break even with their investment and to profit on their products.

Try using a freemium app right now and chances are, before you even reach the app landing or homepage, an ad will pop out or an ad banner will appear. Whenever you see the ads, the developer of that app gets a cut from the advertiser.

If you have an app that users open and use frequently, you have a high potential to get many ad views which translates to more ad revenues for you. Mobile advertising is now becoming more robust and app developers often come out as big winners in this advertising arrangement.

- **Global revenues from freemium apps are rising.** According to App Annie Intelligence – an app analytics firm, global revenues for free apps in the Apple App Store have quadrupled in the past two years. For Google Play apps, it has risen at least thrice in the same period. In fact, free apps take up 69% of all global iOS app revenues while the figure is 75% for Android.

The revenues are of course from mobile advertisements, and this point only reinforces the one mentioned above. More app users are now accepting mobile ads as a way of life or kind of like a tradeoff for being able to download a highquality app for free. As long as the ad is integrated in such a way that it doesn't affect the functionality of the app, people may be willing to overlook these ads.

- **People are more compelled to download free apps.** For app users, paying for an app can be a gamble, especially if they're only basing their purchase on reviews and screenshots. There is no way to know whether an app is worth its price until after it has been downloaded.

Also keep in mind that app purchases are transacted using credit cards. Once an app is purchased and downloaded, the activity is automatically considered as a complete transaction. If in the event the user is disappointed with the app, they have the option to ask for a refund. Unfortunately, the refunding process is not as quick or automatic as making a purchase.

For the App Store, if Apple considers your reason for asking for a refund is valid, it can take up to a week before the amount is reimbursed. For Google Play, if the refund was requested within 15 minutes of downloading it, the refund will be processed immediately. After the grace period however, it becomes tricky.

Because of these procedures in place, it is understandable that people are more wary of paying for new apps that are not as publicized or reviewed as other premium apps. This is obviously an advantage for freemium apps since it makes it easy for users to download and test out the app with no commitments or strings attached.

- **Why pirate something you can get for free?** As in creative products in the technology and communication industries, piracy is a big problem. Believe it or not, there are plenty of ways that apps are pirated so that other users can access it for free.

Most, if not all the apps that are pirated are the ones that aren't free which makes sense, because why would anyone invest resources in illegally recopying apps that anyone can download without having to pay for it.

With a free app, you won't have to worry about piracy. Illegal copies of your app won't be making its rounds which mean that you still have complete control over the aspects of your product such as updates and advertising on the apps that users will download from legitimate app stores.

There are a lot of developers who use the freemium app model in order to profit from their products. However, publishing free apps isn't perfect either. Let's now look at the disadvantages of releasing apps for free download.

Disadvantages of Free Apps

You'd be hard pressed to find smartphone users who don't appreciate free stuff but even with an enthusiastic market for your app, publishing a free product isn't always good for your bottom line. Let's look at several disadvantages to releasing the "freemium" apps:

> • **Mobile advertising does not guarantee profits.** Earlier, we mentioned how mobile advertising helped free apps profit more than paid ones. But what wasn't mentioned is that it takes a whole lot more than just placing ads on an app in order to get a piece of advertising revenue.

Most mobile advertising agencies require a minimum number of impressions, actions or clicks. For example, an advertiser may offer $0.70 per 1,000 ad impressions. So in order for you to make decent money, you need to ensure that the users of your app will frequently and regularly launch your app so that they can see the ads.

Now what if your app isn't exactly something that needs to be used on a daily basis say like a first aid manual for home use for example? Unless minor accident happens regularly (knock on wood), it's difficult to assume that users will refer to the app frequently. Without users launching your app as a habit, your ad metrics will suffer.

Unless you have an app that is guaranteed to be instrumental in the daily routine of its users – whether it's something they use for productivity or for entertainment, publishing a free app may not be the route you want to take if you want to make money in this industry.

- **Free apps don't always have a good impression.** Yes people love free things but there is also a lot of believers of the saying "you get what you pay for". In the case of mobile apps, there is a large volume of low-quality free apps that makes smartphone users willing to shell out a few dollars for something they know will be worth it.

Unfortunately, when you release your free app, users won't have an idea of how well it works. The only things they have as references are screenshots of your app and your description. Reviews are also important for app users but you won't always have those as soon as you launch your app in an apps store.

You will have to prove to app users that your app is worth their time and download. More importantly, you have to show that your app is worth keeping on their smartphone. It is very easy for a free app to get deleted and uninstalled. Your challenge is to make your app the best it can be to make it a favorite among your customers.

- **Advertisements aren't always appreciated.** Let's face it, advertisements aren't always something that anyone is excited to see, maybe unless it's a Superbowl ad. The same aversion is present with mobile ads, especially if it affects the app's functionalities and how the users interact with the app.

Most mobile advertising companies allow developers full control of how the ads will appear. Whether it's a full-screen ad or just something inconspicuous at the bottom of the screen, it's all up to the developer. This is an important point if you are looking to monetize free apps. You'll need to test out different ad layouts to see which one is the least intrusive.

Most people will not mind an advertisement that doesn't affect the usability of the app. This way, your mobile ad metrics won't suffer and the users of your app won't get annoyed with your monetization strategy.

- **App clutter.** You may have seen smartphones that have so many apps that searching for one manually takes a bit of time and effort. App clutter is a very common problem for smartphone users.

So how does this affect free apps? Imagine having your own app clutter problem. In order to better organize your UI, you might need to do some purging. Which of the apps will you get rid of first? Chances are, the apps that are rarely used will be the first ones to go and more likely than not, these are the free apps that the user downloaded.

Free apps are very easy to uninstall because the user did not pay for its download. There will be very few regrets in deleting free apps that are rarely used. People are more wary about under using paid apps because they want to get the value for their money.

To avoid this, you'll need to have an app that people love and need. Even a simple alarm clock app or shopping list app can be something that smartphone users rely on to increase their productivity. This will make your app more "sticky" and less likely to get uninstalled.

It is possible to make more money through mobile advertising on free apps, but there are also disadvantages to this app development model. In the next section, we will be looking at the different end of the spectrum – advantages and disadvantages of launching paid apps.

Advantages of Paid Apps

There are only a little over 140,000 paid apps in Google Play. A stark contrast from Apple's.

What remains to be seen from these figures is that free apps reign supreme in the two biggest app stores for smartphones. The question now is, should you still consider launching your app as a product with a price tag?

Let's look at the advantages of paid apps:

- **Predictable revenue.** If free apps rely on advertisers for revenue, paid apps rely on its quality. If the app is of premium quality, it will have an excellent chance of having good sales so long as other variables of the equation are also making strides in progress (marketing, reviews, etc.)

Not all free apps get downloaded and used in decent numbers to make a dent in advertising expectations. This greatly affects the developers' ability to make a decent income out of their apps. Paid apps on the other hand deliver income to its developers before they are even launched by the users.

This model ensures that you will get your revenue without being at the mercy of how often your app is used. You won't have to rely on ad impressions, clicks or installs in order to make money.

It will be easier for you to make marketing plans and other promotion strategies according to your sales metrics – something that you have full access to as purchases are made.

- **Greater revenue.** Taking our case study example in an earlier chapter, Doodle Jump made $2.8 million in app revenues on iOS alone, even with a price tag of just $0.99 per download. That's approximately a million downloads worldwide.

Truth of the matter is that this kind of revenue cannot be guaranteed with mere ad impressions and clicks. If you developed a high quality app that people will love and enjoy, you can get great reviews and possibly free promotion from the app stores themselves. This can greatly boost your app sales and even with a price of less than a dollar, it can all add up to millions – something that plenty of different paid apps have achieved in the past two to three years.

- **Preferential treatment.** Most (if not all) app stores will naturally prefer paid apps over free ones for the simple reason that it is where they earn money. Unless free app developers uses sponsored advertisements from iAd for Apple or AdMobs for Google Play, the app stores will not be able to get a share from ad revenues from free apps.

To prove this preferential treatment, all you'll need to do is to go to any app store and see which top rated apps list you notice first – the paid apps or the free ones? The paid apps are always listed on the top of the app store homepage, under the recommended or editor's choices. This makes it easier for users to be wowed and allured by the apps that cost money first, before the ones that they won't have to pay for.

This also gives paid apps a better chance of competing with free ones. After all, not everyone is enthusiastic about shelling out yet more money after purchasing an expensive smartphone or tablet. This subtle app store layout greatly helps developers who release their apps for paid downloads.

- **Ad-free environment.** One advantage that users have with paid apps is that they won't have to deal with pesky advertisements anytime they do something on the app. This is also the reason why developers opt to release free versions of their app with mobile ads and another paid, ad-free version.

This is a common practice among app developers and you would do well to follow this strategy. There are smartphone users who are willing to shell out a few bucks just to enjoy their apps without advertisements popping in and out.

- **"Stickiness".** As mentioned earlier, inactive free apps are easier to uninstall that paid apps. Refunding app purchases is not easy, something that is advantageous to developers who launch their apps to be bought.

Disadvantages of Paid Apps

Paid apps aren't always as glamorous or lucrative as it sounds. Let's look at its disadvantages and how to address them.

- **Higher expectations.** A crux of paid apps is that people automatically expect it to be top notch. Because of this expectation, people who did pay money to buy your app will not be so forgiving if they are disappointed. People want to get their money's worth and if you are able to deliver more than what is expected, you will get five-star reviews and raves from your customers.

A great app that people will want to purchase has elements of utility, visual appeal, functionality and a myriad of features. If you are able to deliver these elements for a reasonable price, you could very well reach your target revenue in a short amount of time.

- **Platform's portions.** Again, we mentioned earlier that app stores take a cut out of every app sale. The big four platforms deduct 30% of the app price though Windows Mobile reduce the percentage to 20% after an app reaches the quota of $25,000 in sales.

To some developers, 30% does not seem like a nominal amount but once your app starts selling, it does add up. Let's use an example:

An app that is selling for $1.99 in Google Play will yield a $1.39 per sale for the developer. Doesn't seem too bad right? Now let's say that the app sold 10,000 copies over the span of six months. The developer should expect to receive paychecks that will amount to $13,900. But without the 30% deduction, he would have received $19,900. That's a difference of $6,000 or $1,000 per month.

The app store percentages are a necessary evil. After all, paid apps do get special treatment compared to free apps. You can make up for the losses by selling more copies of your app and if it's something that people rave about, it won't be too difficult to profit from your initial investment.

- **Payouts and thresholds.** We already discussed payments and thresholds of app stores earlier but we also need to mention the specifics of the payout schedules and its thresholds:

Apple App Store – Apple has a payment threshold of $150 with a monthly payment schedule, typically at the start of each month. The payouts that you receive are for sales from a month before or more. For example, the payout that you receive in March could be from your sales from January.

Google Play – Android recently extended its payout period to 15 days after the end of each month. It has a low payment threshold of $1.

Windows Mobile Marketplace – there is a payment threshold of $200. It could be sales for one app or the cumulative sales of all your apps in the Marketplace. Windows does not clarify its payout schedules in its app developer resource materials but it does mention that payouts occur in monthly cycles.

üü **BlackBerry App World** – BlackBerry has a payment threshold of $50 payable monthly. The company does not specify when the payment cycle begins and ends. For sales below the threshold, the amount will be carried over to the next month's payout cycle.

Waiting for payouts is often one of the most complained about part in mobile app development. Let's say that your $0.99 app was launched on the App Store on January and only sells 10 copies on its first month, another 100 on February and 300 copies on March. You'll only receive your revenue at the end of April or early May and only $284 instead of $405 after Apple takes its cut.

This is one major reason why developers opt to launch their apps for free and just monetize it using mobile advertisements. Less successful paid app developers have had to wait months before they were able to receive payments for their sales, which directly affects their ability to break even with their investment.

- **The apps that do well are those on the charts.** Unfortunately, the competition for developers becomes all the more condensed with paid apps. Even if the app prices are relatively cheap, people are still apprehensive with pressing the 'Buy' button. For this reason, the apps that are highly-rated or most downloaded get a leg up on its competitors.

If you look at the different app store layouts, you'll see charts and lists of the most downloaded, most rated or recommended apps on its splash page. Immediately, the smartphone users are given suggestions on what apps are being bought and downloaded the most. The power of suggestions gives these apps an advantage. The higher your ranking is in the charts, the higher the likelihood that it will be purchased.

But what if your app isn't on these charts? Or what if your app isn't featured on the homepage like Benny Hsu's Photo-365 was? It will be a hard climb up but if you are confident in your product's capability to please smartphone users, you'll have a fighting chance to have your app in the charts as well.

- **App sales fluctuates.** It is not uncommon for apps to start out strong in app sales and then see the sales dwindle over time. Truth is, the app market is fickle and the people that go to app stores are always looking for the latest craze. Over time, your sales will start to lag behind other newer apps unless you are able to sustain your brand through marketing, promotions and/or upgrades.

With paid apps, you can't afford to rest on your initial success. You'll need to continually build on your product, fix bugs, add features and offer updates to keep your customers happy. The happier they are, the better your reviews will be and they will be more inclined to recommend the app to their networks.

7. Tips on Choosing App Type and Content

It's not easy to decide which app type to choose. On top of that you also need to plan out what your app will be all about. The preparation phase is typically the most difficult and perplexing part of app development, but it also the most important. In this section, we'll give you some tips and techniques to make the app type and content selection process a bit easier.

- **List down want you want your app to do.** This is probably one of the first considerations that you'll need to make. If you want an app that can be used offline and make reminders to the user, a mobile app will not be capable of delivering those features. Listing the functionalities that you want your app to have will help you in determining the best and most appropriate app type.

- **Identify your target market.** As in any business endeavor, you need to know who you're making your app for. Identifying a demographic is essential if you want clear direction when making plans for your app. Consider the age group, location, gender and app usage of your market when researching demographics.

- **Get to know your target market.** Now that you know who you're making an app for, the next step is to get to know them more. What are their app usage habits? How much are they willing to pay for quality apps? What kinds of features and functionalities do they want in an app? This will help you fine-tune your app so that you can provide the wants and needs of your market.

- **Your competition.** Do a sweeping research of apps that have a similar style or content to what you're planning to develop. Observe their UIs, features and capabilities, as well as their short-comings that you can include in your app. Check out all similar apps on all app stores. Another observation you must make is the number of people who have downloaded the apps to see if you're entering a viable and profitable market.

• **Read reviews.** Reviews are perhaps one of the most essential free resources that you have access to when researching about your competition and your market. The reviews typically mention what users love about the app and what wasn't working for them. This is valuable information that you can use to make your app better than what is available on the app stores at the moment.

Look for complaints relating to the app's performance and content and see if you can improve on those by prepping and adding more content or by using a different app type.

• **Consider the trends.** When doing your research on app stores, also pay close attention to what is trending. You can also narrow down your search to categories to see what types of apps are the top rated – what kind of functionalities do they have and what type of market they serve. If you are planning to release a paid app, check out the rankings and the prices of the apps are sold.

• **What's your budget?** Of course, it will be difficult to do this project without any type of budget constraints. Otherwise, you may find it more difficult to profit or even to breakeven on your app. Even the grandest ambitions for an app can be brought to its knees by a small budget so choose your app type carefully.

In the next chapter, we will discuss your app development options and you'll find out more about how you can maximize your budget without sacrificing quality.

There is no set formula on what is the best combination of app type and content. Plotting out different possibilities can help you determine which app type will be the most optimal for your content. Proper and diligent planning is the key to ensuring that the next stages of the development process will go as efficiently as possible.

8. Getting Started – App Development Basics

Once your done creating the blueprint for your app, it's now time to get the coding part started. If you have never programmed an app before, you have two options: use a web-based app builder or outsource the work to an experienced developer.

We will be looking at both options more closely and we'll begin with a common practice among first-time app producers - outsourcing.

Outsourcing

Outsourcing is not uncommon in the app development world. Not everyone who has a great app idea is capable of writing lines upon lines of code that will produce an app that looks and acts the way it was intended to. Instead of investing in app programming courses, the practical route to take is to hire someone who has the knowledge and skill to do what you can't. Let's look at the different ways to get you started in your search for the right partners for your project.

Finding the Right Developer

There are online communities where you'll be able to find the right developer for your app. In fact, you may be able to find hundreds of developers who will be willing to work with you. Unfortunately, finding the right person for the job isn't as easy as finding someone who has the ability to do what you need to be done.

Different developers have different areas of specialization, going rates, working habits and experience. The last thing you want is for your app's launch date to get repeatedly pushed back because of a developer's inability to deliver the goods or because you have butted heads with your partner/s in the middle of the project. Follow these tips and guidelines so that you can avoid these potentially disastrous situations:

- **Look for developers in reputable online job posting sites.** There are plenty of job listing websites where you can post your requirements. These websites have safeguards in place to ensure that you're not getting ripped off by pretend developers.

There is a dedicated section in this chapter for these websites so that you invite real app developers to join you in your endeavor without having to worry about getting your money's worth.

- **Always state all project variables before any work is done.** Before handpicking the developer/s you want to work with, be sure that they know everything there is to know about the app that you want them to do. Here are some examples of things that your prospective developer must know before you select them:

Who will be designing the GUI of the app? Do they need to provide mockups for you? If so, how many studies will you require?

What app type will you need programmed – native, mobile or hybrid? Which platform and app store will the app be launched at?

What functionalities and features will be included in the app? Does it need a multi-touch capability? Will an internet connection be required? Will the app use any of the phone's functions like the camera or location services?

When are you planning to have the app up and running and ready to be released?

Are there other app developers working on the project? If so, how are you planning to divide the work?

The developer may also ask questions about the specifics of your planned app to see whether they are capable of delivering the product according to your expectations. It is always better to learn early on whether a person will be able to work on ALL your requirements rather than discover this midway.

In line with this, you'll need to have a **non-disclosure agreement** with all the developers who will know about the details of your project. A non-disclosure agreement is essentially a contract between you and the people you interview that prohibits them from revealing any details about what you and he/she discussed to any other people.

This protects your ideas from being used without your approval in the event that you choose a different developer to work with. An electronic document is typically used though a simple e-mail will do. Make sure that the other person agrees to the non-disclosure agreement BEFORE you discuss any specific details about your project.

- **Be clear about your budget.** Always discuss your budget for your project to all your prospective developers before choosing one. This point also reinforces the last because the depth of work that needs to be put in to program your app will also affect how much money the developer will ask for. Be sure to discuss money matters before choosing a developer so that you won't have to stop in the middle of the programming process because of disputes.

This also includes payment arrangements. Will you pay the developer outright before the project begins? Will the payments be made on a weekly or monthly basis? Will you pay the developer only after the app is finished? As pessimistic as it sounds, money can come between a good working relationship between colleagues and in the end, it's the product that suffers. Avoid all this drama by getting out of the way as soon as possible.

- **Experience counts.** When posting your project for bidding, you may get tempted with the offer of developers to work on your app for a fraction of the cost. Though budgetwise this will be good for you, you also need to know why these developers are offering their services at a lower cost than the others.

More often than not, it's because these developers have less experience in app programming. It doesn't always follow that inexperienced developers will not be able to deliver. You also need to look at what you need them to do. If it's a simple web app, maybe a rookie developer will be able to do it. On the other hand, if it's a complex native app with a myriad of features, you may be better off with the more expensive yet more experienced developers.

You can also ask for a portfolio or sample of the developers' previous projects. See if they have a good collection of apps that they programmed themselves to get a better idea of their skills. Though app development isn't exactly a decadeold trade, it still helps to have years of experience in programming apps and other software.

- **Ask about their development process.** App creation isn't just a one-step coding process. It involves preparation for both you and the developer. So if you hear a developer say that they "begin coding ASAP", then you should ask more questions or better yet, look for someone else.

A good developer is not only skilled in what they do; they also organize their process to make it easier for their clients to understand their progress. They should be able to provide project milestones, a schedule of what should already be accomplished by a certain period, and other cues to gauge how far along the project you guys are.

- **Documentations.** A professional developer will always provide details of what they will be bringing to the table. It doesn't have to be a formal invoice with logos (though it is a plus), just a formal acknowledgement that lists all the work that they are expected to deliver. They can also provide additional documentation as each stage of the process is completed.

You should also provide the developer with a list of things that you expect them do. Have the developer electronically sign this document so that you have something in black and white to show in the event that the developer fails to deliver an aspect of the app that you both agreed on.

The documents are like the framework of the entire project, a formal to-do list if you will, or something that you and your developer can refer to at any point during the project duration. It also protects both of you should a dispute arise in the future.

Ask the developers whether they provide project documentations before you start working with them. Someone who doesn't keep track of what they do might not be able to give you the value for your money.

• **Clear lines of communication.** It is of utmost importance that you are able to communicate with your developer. It's not enough that you are able to get on the same page before the project goes underway, you also need to ensure that you'll be able to reach them at any stage of the project.

A developer can suddenly go MIA for a wide variety of reasons and this may cause delays and extra costs on your end. You'll need to be very clear with the developer that you have communication requirements (like e-mail replies after 48 hours), taking into consideration applicable time difference.

You can also schedule weekly meetings online so that you can get an update on how the app is coming along. This will make it easy for the both of you to discuss any concerns about the project.

• **Warranties.** No app is developed perfect the first time. Chances are, there will be bugs and minor inconsistencies right after the app is finished. You need to know whether the developer will take responsibility for these bugs even after you have released their payments.

You need a developer who will be able to guarantee that they will be around to fix all that needs fixing, at least until a month or two after the project is officially finished. This will give you enough time to test out the app to find other bugs and flaws.

It is important that you have a warranty from the developer. Otherwise, you'll need to find another developer who will be able to fix the errors, something that may actually take more time than creating an app from scratch.

Don't rush yourself in finding an app developer. You should be very critical of the people that you work with. Don't be afraid to ask questions. After all, this app is your product, brand and source of income – you shouldn't settle for anything less than the best.

9. Where to Find Developers

After making thoughtful considerations on what type of developer to look for, it's time to know *where* to find them. Not all people have the luxury of being best friends with talented app developers. For the majority of us, we need to rely on job posting websites to find the right developers for our project.

Here are some of the best job listing and project bidding websites that you can use:

Elance

Elance is one of the biggest and most popular online meeting places for business owners and freelancers. This website lets businesses and companies post jobs and specific tasks that they need to outsource.

How Does It Work?

To find freelancers, all you'll need to do is to create and register an account on Elance then create a job listing. There are plenty of job templates that you can use to create your ad.

Once you have posted your job, freelancers will then make proposals for the task. Applicants will provide you with their credentials and their proposed rates to get the job done. You will be able to screen the applicants and if needed, ask for additional documentation like portfolios or links to their past work.

When posting a job, you need to include details about the task and how freelancers will be compensated (hourly, monthly or other arrangements), how long the project will last, as well as your minimum requirement for applicants.

Posting jobs is free of charge and you can post as many jobs as you want. However, Elance deducts an 8.75% service fee from the rates that you and your chosen freelancer agreed to. This deduction is taken as a commission from your payment through the site's payment facility and takes place before the money is transferred to the freelancer's account.

For example, you and your freelancer agreed to a bulk payment of $800 after the project is completed and you're about to make the payment. You'll deposit the $800 to the Elance payment facility and it will transfer the payment to the freelancer's account. Before it does however, $70 will be deducted as commission and the freelancer will receive $730 in their account.

Advantages of Using Elance

A lot of individual professionals and companies swear by the usefulness of Elance when it comes to connecting them with skilled freelancers. It has one of the biggest networks of freelancers and skilled professionals which make it easy to find the right person for the job.

Elance also pays special attention to job qualifications. The site has its certification courses to gauge the skills of freelancers. The site also helps ensure that only applicants that qualify according to your requirements will be able to submit a proposal.

The feedback system also helps in providing additional information about the applicants. It is a straightforward five-star system that rates an individual according to the quality of their work, their knowledge in their field, their cost, their work schedule and professionalism.

The site also has excellent security systems in place to avoid fraud. Elance will hold any payment transfers to freelancers until agreed upon milestones are met. There is also a dispute center that handles arguments between freelancers and the people that hired them. Disputes are handled with utmost professionalism and are settled after the submission of evidences from both sides.

Disadvantages of Using Elance

One of the main drawbacks of Elance (and other job listing sites for freelancers) is that you will mostly find people who are at the beginning of their careers. This is especially true now with the unemployment situation in the country. If you want to work with the absolute best, you might have better luck looking elsewhere.

Though not completely the fault of Elance, freelancers do have the reputation of missing milestones and deadlines. Unfortunately, this is beyond the site's purview and you'll have to deal with delays by discussing the issue with your freelancer.

You are also forbidden from posting or asking for specific personal details such as phone numbers, Skype usernames and other information that would allow direct communication outside of Elance. You are also prohibited from making payment arrangements outside the site. This can become a problem down the line for complex multi-faceted projects that involves other freelancers or professionals.

GetAppsDone

GetAppsDone is a job listing site specifically for mobile apps. It started out as job posting site for iOS apps but has since expanded to all platforms.

How does it Work?

Much like Elance, GetAppsDone connects employers to app developers with its job directory. Creating an employer account is free and you can immediately begin posting jobs after you activate your account.

To post a job, you'll have to fill out a simple form detailing the type of work that you need. This is also where you'll be able to state the payment arrangement between you and the freelancers, as well as the app platform that you need programmed.

It is a free service as of the moment and GetAppsDone does not take a pay cut for finished projects. You will also be able to exchange contact information with your freelancer and arrange compensation without having to go through the site.

Advantages of Using GetAppsDone

The main advantage of using this site is its focus on app development. All the freelancers in GetAppsDone have skills related to creating an app so you won't have to sift through hundreds of applicants to find the one that matches all your requirements.

Using GetAppsDone is still free so any completed projects posted on the site won't require a service charge or commission.

Disadvantages of Using GetAppsDone

GetAppsDone is relatively new in the online job posting industry so don't expect the same glut of developers scrambling to apply to your job listing. It also doesn't have the same feedback system and qualification requirement for freelancers so you might get a mixed bag of applicants ranging from the beginner coder to the experienced.

Behance

Behance is the premier job listing site for creative professionals that connects them with employers who are looking to utilize their skills. App programming is one of the categories that are becoming more popular with freelancers and employers alike.

How does it Work?
To post a job, you have the option to either purchase a single posting or multiple posts. The price for posting one job is $199, for five jobs it's $899 and for 10 it's $1,699.

Once you have paid the posting fees, you will be able to specify the details of the job you want outsourced. Freelancers and professionals will be able to send in their application along with their portfolio links, resumes and cover letter. The rates are determined by you and there's no need for applicants to name their price.

Your job listing will be active for 60 days and people can send in their applications throughout this period. You can also end the listing early if you already have a freelancer you want to hire.

Advantages of Using Behance

Many employers are put off by the job listing fee but if you are looking for creative professionals for big projects, the $199 per job posting is actually cheaper than a commission according to a percentage like Elance's model.

Behance is more than just a job search website. It is also a community where artists, writers and developers can upload their projects and have their peers comment on their work. Employers can also browse through uploaded portfolios and offer jobs to the person directly.

Over 1,000 people sign up for a Behance account every day, making the site the biggest melting pot of creative professionals. Unlike the certification efforts of Elance, Behance lets the artists' work speak for their own qualifications so you'll know what kind of output to expect from the applicants of your post.

Disadvantages of Using Behance

When choosing to work with a freelancer on Behance, you are essentially taking a leap of faith. After you have posted your job and selected the person you want to work with, it's basically all up to the both of you to hash out the details of the project – including deadlines, milestones and payment arrangements.

Behance has no control over their members after they have been selected for a project. You can leave feedback for the freelancer or professional but the site has no provisions for disputes between the employer and their employee. If in the event your freelancer misses deadlines and milestones, Behance has little authority to intervene.

10. Common Mistakes to Avoid When Outsourcing

Before you start posting your app coding job on the websites mentioned in the previous section, you have to bear in mind that outsourcing comes with risks. Although you can't ascertain what's to happen in the future, there are ways to mitigate these risks to give your project a better chance of succeeding without unnecessary hiccups along the way.

Be careful of low rates and "friendly" discounts. Unless it's a real friend offering you discounts, you should be wary of complete strangers offering to do the job at reduced or super low prices. Try to remember the phrase "you get what you pay for" when outsourcing work. Very low bids for your business can be a sign that they don't understand how extensive your project is or they might not be experienced in their field of work.

Agreeing to only a single work submission. There are freelancers who would try to submit only the completed work and not milestones in between. This is something that you should not agree to at all costs. It will be difficult to know the actual progress of your app based on worded updates only. Seeing how the programming work is progressing will let you know if your project is on the right track. It also saves you time on modifications later on, which in turn will save you money.

Paying in advance. Though making an advance payment may seem like a good faith gesture, you have no assurance that your money will be put to good use. The risk of having a freelancer bail on your project with your money outweighs its benefits. If a freelancer asks for an advance or down payment, you may want to scout other programmers.

Communication barriers. Needless to say, you'll need a stable channel of communication with your app developer at ALL stages of the programming process, even after the work is finished. If you're still in the interview stage with a freelancer and they're already showing signs of unpredictability when it comes to exchanging ideas or simply getting in touch, you may want to avoid dealing with them as much as possible.

Always ask for ALL the app files. Once the coding is finished, the developer should provide you with a copy of all the files that was created or used. You are the legal owner of these files and the developer should turn all of these over to you even before you give them the final payment.

Get all the legal agreements straightened out before starting. Legal agreements don't have to be super formal but they are of utmost importance. Aside from a non-disclosure agreement, you also need to have the developer sign a copyright agreement stating that you are the rightful owner of the app and all materials relating to the app and that the developer cannot use these materials for any personal, professional or commercial gain without your consent.

You may also want to create agreements for deadlines, milestones and payment schedules to keep your project on track and on schedule as much as possible.

11. DIY Basic Development

Outsourcing app development isn't your only option if you don't know how to do the coding yourself. You can also use a wide variety of online DIY app making tools for a small fee. These tools are limited though and may not be able to create super elaborate apps. However, if you're planning to create a relatively simple app that's centered more on content than in functionalities, these tools may be the right way to go.

Native Apps

> **AppExpress.** This builder is perfect for small businesses and local enterprises. With AppExpress, you can create an app with invoicing, catalog and scheduling functionalities. It provides templates for you to work with and you can add the features as you go along without having to do any backbreaking programming and coding. This program lets you create iOS and Android apps only.

There is a subscription fee of $75 a month and it does not include licensing fees for publishing the app on app stores.

> **iBuildApp.** iBuildApp has only been around for two years but it has already helped create over 60,000 apps for Android and iOS devices. This builder is more focused on business and company-related apps so it does have its limitations in terms of functionalities.

Creating an app is free with iBuildApp and it has its own submission platform though the licensing and testing fees are excluded from the package. You can also subscribe to their packages beginning at $9.99 per month. You can also pay $299 for iBuildApp's help to create your Apple Developer account and to migrate your app to its store for iOS.

> **AppsBuilder.** This builder is one of the most popular because of its ease-of-use and app success rate with over

8,000 apps published per month. AppBuilder can create apps for Android and iOS with no need for coding knowledge. It also uses a cloud-based system so you'll be able to edit your apps as often as necessary before submitting it to the app stores.

AppsBuilder also has packages starting at €19 a month. It allows a 30-day free trial period for those who want to test out its features and capabilities first.

Mobile Apps

PhoneGap. The mobile app development tool that Wikipedia used for its iOS, Android and Playbook app. PhoneGap allows the development of apps for the following platforms: iOS, Android, Windows Mobile, Bada, BlackBerry and WebOS.

Using PhoneGap to develop an app is free of charge. But there are fees for support plans which start at $24.95 per month or $249.

EachScape. Unlike other online mobile app builders, EachScape has a dragand-drop environment that doesn't rely on ready-made templates. This gives apps a more unique feel that can be easily differentiated from other apps made using the same builder. Aside from developing HTML5 apps, you can also create native apps for iOS and Android using their own languages.

EachScape is pricey but well worth it. Licenses begin from $2,500 per month.

Red Foundry. Developers can create apps with or without coding knowledge. Apps are built in the web-based Fusion Studio or through the more advanced Fusion Elements. Using these builders, you will be able to see and test the app on your device as you are building it. Alternatively, you can also hire Red Foundry developers to create your app for you at competitive prices.

Creating apps using Red Foundry's tools are free. If you need support from the Red Foundry team, packages begin at $199 a month.

Hybrid Apps

Appy Pie. This site uses a drag-and-drop interface that needs no coding, programming or graphic arts skills. Anyone will find it easy to use the tool and you can design and create an app in minutes. You will also have access to realtime app analytics to help you in your promotion or monetization strategies. Signing up is free of charge and you can choose the platform for your HTML5 hybrid app.

You can create your app without paying for anything but fees apply for publishing your app. Rates for publishing begin at $12 a month which includes app submission through Appy Pie.

Tiggzi. Tiggzi is a cloud-based app making tool that requires no downloads or installation. The tool uses a JavaScript-based drag-and-drop interface that makes it easy to connect to third-party APIs and plug-ins. You can begin building an app without having to pay for any subscriptions. You'll be able to export the app as HTML or alternatively you can create a binary for iOS or Android publishing.

You can also pay $40 a month for a Tiggzi builder package which allows more API installations and provides more storage space.

12. App Testing

After completing your app, there's only one more step that needs to be taken before you put your product up for download on app stores. This critical step is something that you can't by-pass and the credibility of you app may very well depend on this. This step is product testing.

App testing can determine whether your app gets approved by app stores for selling. It's also the best time to make modifications to fix whatever needs fixing. There are three ways that you can go about with app testing, you can do a group, a usability testing or both. Let's look at group testing first.

Focus Group Testing

This type of testing involves a group of six to eight people from your target market whose sole purpose is to discuss your app. Give them time to test out and explore your app. After this exercise, ask them questions about what they like or dislike about your app or what they think are its strengths and weaknesses. Be as specific as possible with your questions while still giving them an opportunity to provide all their insights about your product.

Ask about the functionalities, features, visuals, interface content, price and other aspects of your app. This will help you get a good idea of how your market will react to your app and it also gives you a good starting point for making improvements for your product.

The flow of the discussion is entirely up to you. If you have never done a focus group discussion (FGD) before, here are some tips to make your session(s) a success:

> When selecting participants, always ensure that there is a common quality or characteristic that everyone shares. Some examples are iPhone users, single moms under the age of 30 or people who have purchased an app in the past month.

That's where the similarities should end to maintain the diversity of your group. Keep the commonality to one or two characteristics so that you'll be able to get a diverse mix of people which is a more accurate portrayal of your market.

Once you have a list of participants, set a time, venue and date for the session. Always take into account your participants' availability and schedules. Get in touch with them to confirm the meeting details a week before the date to give you time to make changes or to find other participants if needed. Don't forget to send a final reminder to your group a day before the scheduled session.

Before heading out to your FGD, always prepare your materials as early as possible. You may also want to bring refreshments and snacks for your participants, especially if you think that the session will last for hours though discussions typically only last for 90 minutes at the most. You can also give small tokens of appreciation for your participants like gift certificates or gift cards.

For easier reference later on, tape or video record the session. Just be sure to inform your participants that they are being recorded. You may bring this up with them when you invite them to join your FGD so that they are fully aware of what they will be a part of.

One of the most important elements of an FGD is your prepared questions that will facilitate the discussion. A good FGD facilitator ensures that all the participants feel comfortable about revealing their opinions about the topic. The facilitator should ask probing, one-dimensional questions that will give the discussion a more natural and engaging flow.

So what types of questions should you ask? Here's a short guide:

Opening Questions. These questions make people feel comfortable about being a participant. Make these questions easy to answer but don't let them emphasize the participants' individual differences too much.

Example: *"What is your name and how long have you been using your iPhone?"*

Introductory Questions. These questions introduce the topic to be discussed and helps establish the focus of the dialogues.

Example: *"Upon hearing the app title/name, what's the first thing that comes into mind?"*

Transition Questions. Connects the introductory questions and the key questions. It also expands on the participants' answer to the introductory questions.

Example: *"With those ideas in mind, would you have downloaded the app if it was free? How about if it was a paid app?"*

Key Questions. Focuses on the main topic and purpose of the FGD. This period of questioning should get the majority of the time that you allotted for the discussion.

Example: *"What are your opinions on the graphics and visuals of the app?"*

Closing Questions. Ends the FGD.

Example: *"Were there any topics we missed that you wish to discuss?"*

The flow and order of the questioning is called the "questioning route". A good questioning route always goes from the general to the specific, and always maintaining a light, comfortable tone that will encourage the participants to answer the questions with enthusiasm.

As a moderator of the discussion, it's your responsibility to facilitate the dialogues within the group. A good moderator has these key characteristics:

Confidence. Talk clearly and concisely while maintaining an engaging and friendly tone. Always maintain good posture and most importantly, don't forget to smile and keep eye contact with the participants when addressing them.

Respectfulness. A good moderator knows that all the participants have something to contribute to the discussion. You'll need to treat everyone with equal respect without showing favoritism towards a couple of people in the group.

A good, active listener. Your participants have taken the time and effort to help you by joining your FGD. You need to show your appreciation and gratitude by listening intently and actively to their opinions and ideas.

Neutrality. Remember that this FGD is about your product and the participants' opinions and ideas. There is a time and place for you to share your personal opinions and beliefs, unfortunately an FGD is not it. Always stay neutral and keep the discussion focused on your app.

After the FGD, you'll need to make sense of the data you just gathered. The next step is to analyze the ideas and opinions that your participants shared with you. Analyzing group data has three steps:

Indexing. This process involves transcribing the discussion, organizing data and labeling ideas that are relevant or similar to each other.

Management. After indexing your data, grouping together similar labels are next. There are three ways to manage information: by cutting apart individual responses, electronically cut and paste information to create clusters of data or by using specialized software for qualitative data.

Interpretation. This step is where you'll make sense of the data you just organized. Create summaries for every label or cluster that you have created and then gather these summaries into one cohesive report.

An FGD is extremely useful in getting first-hand feedback from a representation of the population that you're planning to market your app to. However, you need to be aware that it is completely possible for your participants to be swayed by each other's opinions which mean that the feedback that you get is not always 100% reliable.

Take note that the flow of the FGD is entirely up to you. Use the information above as guidelines on how to create your own FGD program. Feel free to add or subtract parts that you believe will make your session more interactive and more conducive to sharing of ideas.

Usability Testing

If a focus group discussion has six to eight participants in one room simultaneously, a usability testing uses a one-to-one approach between a participant and a facilitator.

For app testing, a participant will be given ample time using the app. They will be able to get a full experience of the app's UI, functionalities and features. After the allotted time, the facilitator will ask a series of questions to get the participant's opinions and ideas about the app.

Usability testing is considered as a "black box" testing technique with the objective of discovering errors and bugs that app might have. As a participant interacts with the app, the facilitator will observe several app performance elements, as well as the user's reactions to the app.

Elements to be measured include:

Performance. How many steps did it take for the user to complete basic tasks? How long was the load time of the app from function to function (Example:
loading of pages and screens, loading off the app)

Accuracy. Is the app doing what it is intended to do when prompted?

Memorability. How much of the app's elements and functions does the participant remember after not using the app for a certain duration?

Errors. How many errors did participants receive? What were they doing when these errors appeared? Was it easy or difficult for the participants to recover from the error?

Emotional Response. How does the participant feel when using that app? Does the app relax them or stress them out? Would they recommend the app to their friends and family?

In order to carry out a usability testing, you'll need a fully working prototype installed in smartphones. You can do usability tests at certain points during the app development process. Use your milestones as guides of what to test. This will help you identify areas of improvement as early as possible so you can spend less time and resources correcting these things later on.

Here are additional guidelines for your usability testing sessions:

Have a list of smartphone models that you want to your app to be tested on. It's near impossible to be able to test your app on all models of smartphones so you'll need to research on the ones that the majority of your target market uses.

Consider the venue of your usability testing sessions. Do not restrict yourself to indoor locations or controlled environments. The main purpose of usability testing to see how the app functions and performs in the real world.

If you plan to release your app in several app stores, make sure to conduct tests on all those platforms.

When selecting participants, make it a habit to always ask what phone model they will be bringing.

Feel free to use tools to help you get accurate observations. Bring timers, battery chargers, earphones and other gizmos that you think you will help in your testing sessions.

It goes without saying that usability testing would not be complete with data analysis. Always take down notes of things you observe. Organize your data into clusters that you can use as references for your app's improvements. For example, you can have a cluster for bugs and errors, and another for visual and graphics.

Usability testing typically costs more than focus group discussions in terms of time and money. Despite this, it is absolutely essential in the success of your app. Testing your app is the best way for you and your developer to know how to improve on the app's features and functionalities and it is also the best way to maximize your app's potential.

13. Submitting and Publishing Your App

Congratulations! After a considerable length of time developing and testing your app, you're now ready to start rolling out your product in app stores. In this chapter, you'll learn about the different steps and procedures on publishing your app in different app stores.

Apple App Store

Here is a step-by-step guide for an App Store submission:

1.   Create an Apple Developer account. This is free of charge.

2.   Join the iOS Developer Program. There is a fee of $99 per year.

3.   Create an Identity for your app. You'll only be able to do this as a member of the Developer Program. Go to the iOS Provisioning Portal and click on App IDs then click on the New App ID button. Create a name for your app ID and then give it a Bundle Identifier. Once all fields are completed, click on Submit. You'll be using your Bundle ID in the next step.

4.   Create an iTunes Connect account. This is where you'll be inputting your app's information that will appear on the App Store. Before creating an account however, be sure that you already prepared the following:

   a.   Your app's brief description
   b.   An icon for your app that is 512 pixels by 512 pixels in size

c.   At least one screenshot of your app
d.   Your Bundle ID

Once you got those on hand, go to the <u>Member Center</u> and sign in using your Apple ID and password. Under 'App Store Distribution', click on iTunes Connect and sign in again.

Once signed in, click on 'Manage Your Applications' then click on 'Add New App'. Fill out the information about your app and then click on 'Done' when you're finished.

5.   The next step is to complete the export compliance question. Select 'Manage Your Applications' again on iTunes Connect then select your app. Click on 'View Details' then click on 'Ready to Upload Binary'. Answer the export compliance question then click 'Save' and then click on 'Continue'.

6.   Create a distribution certificate and a private key. You'll be using the Apple Development Center for this step. No matter how many apps you publish, you'll only need one distribution certificate for all of them. Navigate to 'Certificates>Distribution' then go to 'Request Certificate'.

7.   Create a distribution provisioning profile by navigating to the 'Provisioning > Distribution' tab and selecting 'new profile' on the Apple Development Center. Leave the distribution method to 'App Store' then give the profile a name. Select the App ID that you created in Step 3 then create the provisioning profile. You may need to refresh your created profile to appear. Download the profile. You'll need it when you upload your file.

8.   If you need to use push notifications on your app, you'll need an additional certification for that. This certification is app-specific. Go to the iOS Provisioning Portal then go to the App IDs section. Search for the ID that you created in Step 3 then click on 'Configure'. Tick on the box that says 'Enable for Apple Push Notification service'.

9.   The next step is to create an archive and you can do this in two ways. You can either use the Xcode Project Window or App Cloud. You need to archive your app before you can submit it for approval. Make sure that you archive the tested version of your app.

10.   Validate your app's archive by clicking on the 'Validate' button after selecting your archive from the organizer. Sign in using your iTunes Connect credentials then select your app and the right Code Signing Identity. When you're done, click 'Finish'.

11.   Finally, you can now submit your archive to the App Store. In the Archives organizer, choose the archive of your app. Click on 'Distribute' and then select the 'Submit to the App Store' option. Provide your iTunes Connect credentials then click 'Next'. Select your app and the appropriate Code Signing Identity. Enter a filename and location to save your App Store Package.

12.   The last step is to set a launch date for your app. Sign in to iTunes Connect and select 'Manage Your Applications'. Choose your app from the 'iOS App Recent Activity' section then click on 'Rights and Pricing'. Set your launch date, your Price Tier Schedule then click 'Save.

Android's Google Play

If you're planning to release a paid app, create a Google Checkout merchant account first.
Follow these steps to publish your app on Google Play:

1.   Create a Google Play Publisher account. There is a $25 registration fee that you'll pay using Google Checkout.

2. Click on 'Upload Application' then click on 'Browse'. Choose your .apk app then click on 'Upload'.

3. Upload your app's "assets" beginning with the screenshots of your app. Click on the 'Screenshots' field, click on 'Browse' and upload at least two screenshots of your app. After that, upload your icon on the High Resolution Application Icon field. The other fields are optional.

4. Input the listing details. These are the 'Language', 'Title', 'Description', 'Promo Text', 'Application Type', 'Category' and 'Price' fields. If you are publishing a free app, leave the 'Price' field blank.

5. Choose your publishing options. For 'Copy Protection', turning it off means that your app can be downloaded to a device while turning it on means that it can only be downloaded from Google Play and it will require more phone memory to install the app.

Choose your target market for the 'Content Rating' field. To learn more about Google Play's content rating system, click here.

On the 'Location' field, choose All Countries if you want anyone with an Android device to be able to download your app. If you want to publish your app in select territories only, filter the countries on this field

The 'Supported Device' field is where you can select which types of devices can install your app based on the manifest settings from your .apk file. You can also filter problematic devices based on your app testing using this field.

6. Fill out the contact information form.

7. Tick the checkboxes to accept the Android Content Guidelines and United States export laws.

8.   Finally, scroll up to the top of the page and then click on 'Publish'.

Windows Phone Store

To submit a Windows Phone app, follow these steps:

1.   Register an account at the <u>Windows Dev Center</u>. There is a $49 registration fee for individual developers and $99 for businesses and corporations. If you plan on selling your app, you'll need to enter your payout details and a tax profile.

2.   If you want to increase your chances of getting your app approved on your first attempt, follow these optional steps:

   a.   Run the <u>Windows Application Certification Kit</u> to test your app.
   b.   Take screenshots of your app.
   c.   Create a release version of the App Package with the .appxupload file extension.

3.   Go to your Windows Dev Center dashboard. Click on 'Submit an app'. Click on the different fields to accomplish the forms starting with the app name. You don't have to complete these fields in one go though it is advisable for you to save your app name as soon as possible so that it won't be used by anyone else.

After the app name is the 'Selling Details'. Here you'll be able to choose the app pricing, trial details, the release date of your app and other details. Next is the 'Advanced Features' field where you'll be able to detail the special features of your app like push notifications and in-app offers.

You are then to select the age rating and criteria of your app. Bear in mind that your answer here will be cross-checked by Microsoft when it reviews your app. On the next field, answer "yes" if your app uses any form of data encryption.

4.   On the package field, search for your .appxupload on your local files then upload here. You will also be asked for a description of your app. There is also an appropriate field for notes addressed to the app testers.

5.   After submitting your app, Microsoft testers will check if your app meets the compliance guidelines. On your dashboard, you'll see the 'Windows Store Certification' report where it will be determined whether your app passed or failed content compliance.

6.   If your app passed the approval stage, you will receive an e-mail along with a link to where your app can be downloaded by users. If your app failed content compliance, you will be given notes on what you need to fix or modify. You can re-submit your app using the steps above once you have addressed Microsoft's concerns.

Note: You want have to pay the registration fee again. Simply log on to your account and start anew from your dashboard.

14. App Maintenance

Now that you have your app published and ready for download, it's time discuss an important facet of app development: app maintenance.

It's not enough to simply let your app run until the wheels fall off. If you published a paid app, you want to ensure that your customers are satisfied with your product for as long as they have it installed on their smartphones. If you published a free app, you'll want to maintain a steady flow of downloads and you can do that by having an app maintenance plan for your app.

Here are some tips:

• **Think long term.** It's only natural for your app to evolve in the hands of your audience.

App Updates

Before we discuss scheduling your updates, let's first look at how to organize your app versions using numbers.

Check your phone for app updates. You may see update or version numbers like 3.1.2. These numbers are assigned for a reason. These numbers help users and platforms identify what type of update is being done.

The basic number scheme for updates is as follows:

- The first digit is the major version number
- The second digit is the minor release number
- The third digit typically indicates the bug fix version

Using the 3.1.2 example earlier, the number 3 means that it's the third major release, the number 1 indicates that it's the first minor update of the third major release and the number 2 indicates that it's the second bug fix for the first minor release.

Let's use a concrete example. Foursquare, a popular social geo-location app has an update number of 6.0. This basically means that this update is a major version that has some big changes in its features or functionalities. The Adobe Reader app's version number on the other hand is 10.5.2 with the previous version being 10.5.1. This means that only bug fixes and performance enhancements were done and no major changes to the app were made.

The numbers can be confusing in the beginning but it is often necessary to follow this format in order to get the go-signal or approval from a platform's screening process.

Minor Bug Fixes

The most common updates are bug fixes. The bugs may have slipped past you during your testing phase and users were able to catch and report them. These may be hard to schedule because you address them as they are found. That is not to say that you have to release an update for every single bug one after another because it can be costly for you.

You can create a system wherein you address the bugs you receive in a seven day duration, for example. Give those concerns to your developer in bulk so you can save up on the cost. Also bear in mind that app updates also follow the same procedure as app submissions. Having multiple updated versions on queue can complicate your operations. If the bug fix is integral to the functioning of the app, the Apple App Store has a fast-track policy for these types of updates.

Most developers lump together updates and fixes into one release. In order to know which bugs to prioritize, review the number of people affected by these bugs and how severe the problem is.

Bug fixes are essential in ensuring that your app will run as it was intended to. Always read your app reviews and bug reports to stay updated on your app's performance.

Major Updates

An update can be considered major if it involves adding or removing features or changing the UI of the app. This is important if you want to keep your app dated in looks and in function.

Long term planning should be put into the type of major updates that you'll do. Let these tips guide you:

- Pay attention to the feedback of your app's users. Encourage them to write a review about your app to know which parts they like and which parts they want improved.

- If necessary, conduct another FGD or usability test. Invite and interview both frequent and infrequent users of your app to gain an insight of what kinds of updates will improve their experience with your app.
- Check your competitors' apps to see what changes they have made and what their users say about those changes. This is important if you want to stay competitive and up-to-date.

There may come a time when you'll have to remove certain features for various reasons. First, the feature may not be functioning as seamlessly as you expect. Second, the feature may not be something that users utilize and changing it into something more dynamic may be the direction to take.

Try to keep major updates spaced out and avoid rolling out one major update after another. Constant major changes can annoy your users since they'll have to get used to different UI all over again. Constantly having to make big updates can also be time consuming for your users and too much of it might discourage them from updating altogether.

App updates is natural in the life cycle of an app. Good app developers are always in touch with how their users interact with their app and they are always looking for ways to improve the app.

Updates also help in your app's rankings. For iOS apps, updates are also considered in their charts for new apps. If your updates are useful, essential and worth the users' while, their updating may help in the promotion of your app.

15. App Marketing

Whether you published a pay-per-download or a free one, there is always a way to make money off your app.

Use marketing fundamentals to get you started. Prepare high-quality screenshots of your app and create icons and logos to establish your brand. Create a detailed marketing plan that includes schedules and anticipation of your app's performance in app stores.

You'll be a busy bee leading up to the launch of your app but once you have all your materials ready, it'll all be a matter of execution.

In whatever marketing strategy you choose to employ, it's important for you to consider using search engine optimization (SEO) techniques to maximum mileage for your efforts. Here are some basic concepts:

- **Keywords.** Research relevant keywords that you can use in your marketing campaign. Keywords and phrases are essentially what users put in the search fields when they're looking for websites or content about a specific topic.

- **Backlinking.** Backlinking is the practice of providing links within your content that leads to an external website or page.

- **Cross-linking.** Much like backlinking, cross-linking is providing links between two websites or pages. For example, linking your Twitter profile from your Facebook page and vice-versa.

- **Link Exchange.** A common SEO practice where two or more individuals agree to link each other's websites, pages and other content in their own pages. For example, you can strike a deal with a blogger to have their pages linked on your Facebook app page and they will link your page on their blogs.

SEO is very useful in getting your content, website or social media pages on the top of search results. This will make it easier for people to find your online content should they want to learn more about you and your app.

You can use SEO concepts in most online marketing techniques. Create an appropriate SEO strategy for each of your online marketing method.

Social Media Marketing

Social media is one of the most powerful marketing tools that app developers use to promote their apps. Bear in mind that most social networking sites will let you create profiles for your app free of charge, making it one of the most practical and effective strategies you can use.

Facebook, Twitter, Pinterest and Tumblr are the top sites that you should include in your social media marketing. Follow the following tips and guides on how to optimize your app marketing and advertising.

Facebook

Instead of creating a business profile for your app, create a brand page that people can 'Like' and share with their networks. This gives your content an element of "virality" that will make it easier to spread the word about your app.

Here are some useful and effective tips that will help you get the most out of your Facebook page:

- **Decide what your Facebook page is for.** Of course, the most obvious purpose of your Facebook page is to market your app but in what way? Do you want it to be an announcement or news source or would you rather use it as a vehicle to address customers' concerns? Having a clearly defined purpose for your Facebook page will help you make a more efficient and effective Facebook marketing strategy.

• **Customize your page.** There are plenty of ways for you to personalize your Facebook page according to the theme of your app. A good example is Candy Crush Saga's Facebook page. On the cover photo, there are links to make downloading the game easier for iOS and Android users. It also features screenshots and videos of the game on easy to access to tabs.

Personalize your page based on what you want to feature and highlight. The choice is completely up to you!

• **Post regularly.** It's not uncommon for app developers to excitedly create Facebook pages only to see enthusiasm dip within a couple of months. When posts and updates become scarce and far in between, it doesn't give people much of a chance to interact with you and your page. There are plenty of tools that you can use to schedule your posts in advance and it will do the posting for you.

• **Offer incentives to 'Like' your page.** Give people a reason to follow your page and your posts by giving them a reward of sorts for doing so. Whether it's as simple as receiving app updates or something as elaborate as exclusive contests, incentives are effective in building up a good number of followers and building good rapport with your customers.

• **Use analytic tools.** There are plenty of online analytic tools that you can hook up with your Facebook page that can help give you insights on how your marketing strategy is performing. Use these tools to shape your future strategies and to make improvements on your content posting.

There are over 150 million Facebook users in the US alone. Reaching even just 10% of this population can do wonders for your app sales and popularity. With the right strategy and execution, there's no limit to what your Facebook marketing can achieve.

Twitter

Twitter is now one of the most used social networking website worldwide. More and more brands are recognizing the potential of Twitter as a marketing platform because of the ease of sharing content across networks of users.

Consider using Twitter as a supplement to your Facebook marketing campaign. Here are some tips and guidelines for you to remember:

• **Determine your audience.** As in any type of marketing strategy, you need to identify who your target audience is before executing your plans. The same is true for Twitter marketing. Target potential clients, followers of your competitors and potential partners and investors to create a tight plan that gives every tweet a defined purpose.

• **Follow the right people.** The old belief that you should limit the number of people you follow to a handful is no longer general practice, especially when it comes to Twitter marketing. Be strategic in who you follow in Twitter. Influential personalities in your niche or industry are good sources of content and they could be your best promoters for your app.

• **Be engaging.** Twitter is an excellent place for you to interact with your customers. Allot a few hours per day to have light-hearted conversations with your followers. This build a good way to build rapport with your followers and your replies may even get retweeted to their followers.

• **Post useful and unique content.** Any type of content that entertains or catches a user's attention is sure to get retweeted. This is one of the best ways to get your page noticed by more people. Post funny, informative and viral content to get the attention of your followers.

- **Use hashtags strategically.** Over using hashtags can annoy your followers and can get you flagged as a spammer. Only use them as promotion tools or to show support to trending causes. Also limit the number of hashtags you use in a single tweet.

The best way to learn how to use Twitter effectively for marketing your app, check out the Twitter accounts of your competitors or other apps you use. Critic their strengths and weaknesses and bear those in mind when creating your own Twitter marketing strategy.

Google+

Despite failing to overthrow Facebook from the top of the social networking rankings, Google+ is the second most used social media website in the world.

Google+ marketing makes good use of SEO techniques. Here are some easy tips that you can use:

- **Use keywords whenever possible.** Keywords will help get your page a good ranking when people search for those words or phrases. Use keywords on your 'About' page and on content that you post to make it easier for people to land on your page.

- **Post regularly.** Creating a posting schedule for your page and if needed, use third-party tools to automate the posting for you. Don't forget to optimize your posts by including links and keywords.

- **Begin and/or join engaging conversations.** Use your G+ page to encourage conversations and discussions among the people in your circles. This is also a great way for you to get valuable (and free) feedback about your product.

- **Respond to mentions and re-share posts.** Track the mentions that you get and do your best to respond to all of them, even those that criticize your app. This will help connect you to your audience better and to let them know that you value their opinion and patronage of your app.

Business and product pages in G+ are not as plentiful as it is on Facebook so there's still a considerably low number of competition for a share of the users' attention. Take advantage of this and begin your G+ marketing campaign as soon as you can.

Reviews and Blogs

Getting your app reviewed or mentioned in influential blogs can also provide a big boost to your app marketing efforts. You will need to do some research on which blogs and app reviewers to approach with your app.

Let these guidelines help you:

- **Prepare press releases and media kits.** Even before launching your app, prepare press materials that you can easily strategically distribute. Provide images that bloggers and reviewers can post on their sites and of course, a copy of your app. You can also outsource the preparation of these materials. Look for qualified copy and press release writers to make professional kits for you.

- **Create a blog or microsite for your app.** You don't need an elaborate website to feature your app. A simple WordPress or Tumblr site can already provide a good reference site for bloggers and reviewers that you reach out to. There are a lot of free design templates that you can use to pretty up your site. Simply but a domain name to truly personalize your blog or microsite.

- **Don't forget the keywords and phrases.** SEO techniques are especially useful for these marketing types. Use your researched keywords and phrases on your press release and media kits, your write-ups and content of your blog or microsite.

• **Create a unified strategy across different mediums.** Your marketing collateral should have enough variety so that you'll have a content type for every type of medium. Whether it's for print or online publishing, there should be an appropriate type of material that's on-hand and ready for you to distribute.

• **Use with social media.** Tie up your posting schedules or features with your social media accounts so that your followers or fans can share these posts to their networks.

Some bloggers have up to thousands of followers and fans, and a single positive review about your app can go a long way. These bloggers are also respected by their fans as reliable sources of information, and their endorsements and recommendations can boost your app downloads.

Paid Advertisements

Another option for your app marketing is paid promotion. There are several mobile advertising companies for you to choose from like MobClix, AdMob, iAd and TapJoy. The different platforms also typically have their own advertising arm (like iOS' iAd).

The advertising process is pretty straightforward. You'll submit an ad following the size and specifications of the advertising network, you get to determine your budget and how much you're willing to pay for a specific amount of clicks, impressions, downloads or actions. The advertising companies will match your ad with the appropriate apps so that it will appear to the right audience.

If you decide to start a paid advertising campaign, keep in mind these tips and tricks to get you the most bang for your buck:

- **Track, track, track.** It will be very difficult for you to know which of your marketing strategies is pulling in the download and sales numbers unless you use a variety of tracking tools. The key to an effective paid advertising strategy is to have powerful analytics and data to refer to.

Bear in mind that each platform and ad network has its own tracking technology so finding a one-size-fits-all tool will be difficult, if not futile. For every ad network that you pay to advertise your app, make sure that you have a compatible analytics tool to track its performance.

- **Be as targeted as possible.** The biggest ad networks have one thing in common: targeted ad placements. You have the option of specifying your target audience so that you can assure that the right sets of eyes are seeing your ad. Be as detailed as possible when setting the demographics for your ad. Analytics will also play a role here. Track which demographic is converting to downloads the most and adjust your campaign accordingly.

- **Go for simplicity.** Simple ads are easier to make and are unobtrusive. Advertisements don't always have to look like ads. Designs that seamlessly blend into the background will make people more likely to trust its content. Most advertising networks also have character caps so make your copy text concise, brief and witty to attract positive attention.

- **Test your ad.** Have several studies and versions of your ad and conduct a period of testing to see which ones are the best received. On your actual campaign, use these ad versions and match them with the right audience based on your test results and analytics.

- **Have a common theme for your ads.** Aside from mobile ads, you also have the option to have paid advertisements on other places like Facebook or Google. To make your brand easily identifiable, make sure that there is a common theme that ties your ads together. Whether it's the design or copy text, it helps to leave a unifying imprint that would make your ads look professional.

An advertising campaign has its own pros and cons. If you don't have a big advertising budget on-hand, a very targeted campaign would serve you well in delivering additional downloads for your app.

16. App Monetization

Now that your app is in stores and download numbers are beginning to trickle in, it's time to explore your options for making money off your app. This chapter is especially valuable for the developers who are planning to release free versions of their apps.

In-App Advertising

Selling an advertising space on your app is one of the most popular and effective ways to monetize a free app. Based on studies conducted by Interactive Advertising Bureau, mobile advertisers spent $1.6 billion for in-app ads in 2014 alone.

So how does one exactly make money off of other people's ads?

- **Cost-per-click / Pay-per-click (CPC).** You get paid for every click that an ad gets from your app. The going rates for this model vary depending on the advertiser and the advertising network.

- **Cost-per-mille / Cost-per-impression (CPM).** In this model, you get paid for every 1,000 impressions or views the ad gets on your app. You can get anywhere from $0.70 to $5 for every 1,000 views, again depending on the ad network and the advertiser.

- **Cost-per-action (CPA).** Unlike the first two models, this one requires more completed actions from users before it gets added to your metrics. It could be something as simple as liking the advertiser's Facebook page or as complex as completing a survey.

Let's compare the three models to see their pros and cons:

When using advertisements on your app, you need to review the type of app you have in order to match the right method of advertising with your content and features.

Another consideration that you have to look at is the type of ads that you'll be displaying in your app. Here are the ad formats as specified by the Mobile Marketing Association (MMA):

- **Mobile Web Banner.** Web banner ads appear at the top of the screen and can vary in sizes.
o Text tagline banner – Up to 24 characters o Small image banner – 120 x 30 pixels o Medium image banner – 168 x 28 pixels o Large image banner – 216 x 36 pixels o X-Large image banner – 300 x 75 pixels o XX-Large image banner – 320 x 50 pixels

- **Expandable Banners**. Banner ads that can expand to a full-screen view with a tap.

These ads can be a simple static image in JPEG, PNG, GIF and BMP formats or animated GIFS.

- **Interstitial Ad Units.** These are full screen a rich media advertisement that typically appear in between levels of mobile games or while the next app page is loading. It can appear horizontally or vertically depending on the orientation of the smartphone.

- **Video Ads.** These ads typically appear as TV or web commercials and lasts about 30 seconds long. Like interstitial ads, they appear when the app is loading the next page or in-between game levels.

You can choose the formats of ads that you want to appear on your app. Always ensure that the ads don't appear too obtrusive. You also don't want these ads to affect the way users interact or use your app.

Once you've decided to add advertisements to your app, you have a wide range of advertising companies to choose from.

Top Advertising Networks

1.   **Chartboost.** This network is available for iOS and Android apps and you can choose either a CPC or CPI model. Over 12,000 gaming apps are now using Chartboost and is one of the most robust ad networks.

2.   **Tapjoy.** Tapjoy is available for iOS, Android and Windows Phone apps and has a CPI model. It has four available ad formats to choose from and has a reach of 399 million users.

3.   **Flurry.** Only apps for iOS and Android can show Flurry ads. You can choose from three advertising models: CPC, CPM and CPI. Flurry boasts of powerful analytics tools and a reach of over 700 million smartphone and tablet users.

4.   **RevMob.** RevMob is one of the biggest advertising networks for gaming apps. Ads appear on iOS and Android smartphones and use a CPI model.

5.   **AdMob.** Apps on iOS, Android, Windows Phone 7 can carry AdMob ads and it uses a CPC model.

To begin using these ad networks, you'll need to register an account on their sites and set your ad preferences. You'll receive lines of SDK codes that you need to insert on your app's coding.

Most ad networking sites also provide testing environments for you to see what ads will look like when they show up on your app.

In-app advertising is one of the most widely used monetization methods that app developers use. It is a billion dollar industry that many first-time developers hope to tap into.

In-App Purchases

In-app purchases are another method to monetize apps. In this technique, apps are published for free download and revenue is generated through purchases within the apps that improve its game play or expand its features.

Mobile games are the biggest winners in this monetization model though in-app purchases are not limited to that category. Fitness and music apps also benefit from this feature. Paid apps can also offer in-app purchases.

Let's look at the different forms of items that can be sold within iOS apps:

- **Non-consumable.** The item is purchased once and will be available on the account indefinitely like extra or premium content, for example.
- **Consumable.** Items that are lost once used and can be bought as often as the user wants. Typically seen on gaming apps like extra lives or boosts for example.
- **Non-renewing subscription**. Items bought may have an expiration or subscription date and this option requires the user to make another purchase to re-acquire the item.
- **Auto-renewing subscription**. Items or subscriptions are automatically renewed once the subscription expires.

According to Forbes.com, apps that allow in-app purchasing were able to generate the highest revenue per download. This means that the "freemium" model wherein apps are offered free but offer additional items and features for a price is bound to be the most lucrative app monetization model.

The question now is whether you should use the freemium model or not. Let's look at its advantages and benefits:

- It makes the app more accessible to your audience.
- Users are more likely to download free apps, giving you an automatic edge in terms of app viewership.

• In-app revenue gradually builds up as more users become familiar (or addicted) to your app. In contrast, paid app revenues are typically higher near the launch date and gradually slow down.

• If you are able to offer essential items and goods that heightens the quality and functionality of your app, people will be willing to pay a small fee to maintain that.

On the flipside, not all apps do well with the freemium model. Here are some of its disadvantages:

• The people who download free apps are those who are not too excited about parting with their money.

• Most freemium apps have a limited shelf life. This is especially true for gaming apps.

• You'll need to wait longer before sales revenues begin to trickle in. Your audience needs to be engaged with your app first before they feel comfortable about purchasing extra items.

Review your app to see if the freemium model will work for you. Here are some questions for you to reflect on:

• **"Is my app something that people want?"**
The most important factor in making this model work is making sure that your product is something that people want on their smartphone.

• **"What is my distribution cost and reach?"**
The expense of distributing your app should be minimal with the widest reach possible. Assume that only a small percentage of all the users who downloads your app will make an in-app purchase. To make this work for your advantage, you'll need to expand your user base as much as you can.

• **"Who is my market?"**
You also need to take into account the people who will be using your app. If you have an app targeted for toddlers and young children, a freemium model may be a risky choice. Platforms and app stores are

now tightening up their in-app purchasing mechanisms to avoid accidental purchases.

- **"What items do I intend to sell in my app?"**
It would be difficult to breakeven with your investment if you're only selling one or two $0.99 items that won't make a difference on how users will interact or use your app. Make sure the items you sell will enhance your app and will be worth your users' money.

- **"How often will my audience use my app?"**
Is your app something that can be easily integrated into your users' lives? How often will they launch your app?

There is a lot of planning involved when using the freemium model. Even though it has brought a lot of revenue for new developers, there is no guarantee that it will work for every type of app.

Upgrades

Unlike in-app purchases wherein app users have the option to add additional features to improve their experience with the app, upgrading is essentially the option to unlock premium features after trying out a "lite" version.

It is a common practice for app developers to release two versions of their app: a free app with advertising or limited features and a paid, ad-free and full version. A good example of this method is the Livestrong Calorie Tracker app. There is a free, adsupported version of the app with limited features and also a $2.99, ad-free version with complete features.

Let's look at the advantages of offering app upgrades:

- Lite versions are easier to develop than apps with in-app purchasing features.
- Single-function apps don't always have individual items or features to sell in-app.

- Gives users a chance to try and engage with your app before making a purchase.
- App stores have made it easy for customers to upgrade to the premium version by cutting down on the steps to make it possible.

And now for the disadvantages:

- Not all apps have enough content or features to make a lite version without including a considerable amount of premium stuff.
- Since the lite version is free to download, users who are unsatisfied may leave bad reviews without knowing getting the chance to try out the upgraded version.
- You lose the market of users who are willing to purchase the app without testing it first.
- Users might get put off with the required steps to purchase and then re-download the complete version.
- You'll have to create two versions of your app. This means more programming time and cost.

As in any app monetization strategy, there are no set formulas on the best way to go about it. Releasing a lite version does not always guarantee that people will be rushing to upgrade to a premium version. As long as you have your objectives set on what a lite version is supposed to be in the grand scheme of things, you can navigate through this model successfully.

Lite versions are typically used as a marketing tool for the premium versions. Others consider it as an extra monetization method to get a slice of the mobile advertising revenue.

Create a comprehensive game plan on how you want your lite app to function in your overall monetization strategy. Take special note on launch schedules and promotion strategies for each version of your app. Careful planning even before you begin your app development phase will help you in the long run so start planning your monetization schemes as early as possible.

17. Tying Loose Ends

Now you can celebrate, after all you now have an app in app stores with monetization methods set in place!

What's left for you to do is to run a tight ship to ensure that your app download figures keep going strong beyond your launch period. You already know the most fundamental concepts in making money off mobile apps. Simply use what you have learned to create sustainable development, marketing and monetization plans for your app.

And of course, here are some tips:

- **Plan as far ahead as possible.** Even before you begin looking for an app developer or coding your app, write exhaustive plans for the entire lifecycle of your app. Schedule everything in advance. Don't worry, not all plans are always set in stone. Modify your strategy as you go along or as you see fit.

- **Plan with as much detail as possible.** Once you get into app development, you'll realize that you'll be dealing with so many details of different kinds. You'll get so excited that ideas will be crawling out the woodwork. Write these ideas down and if doable, add them to your plans.

- **Be as cohesive as possible.** This is where early and detailed planning will come to fruition. You'll be able to tweak and edit your grand master plan to make every element relevant to each other. For example, your marketing efforts should be closely tied with your monetization method.

A cohesive plan will make it easier for you to maintain your brand and to take it to the next level.

- **Keep learning.** Since this is your first time to develop apps, you still have a lot to learn, even after reading this e-book. The best teacher is experience and there is plenty of experience to be had. Treat every stumble, challenge or mistake as a lesson and don't pressure yourself to get it perfect the first time.

- **Keep going.** There will be lots of times when you'll feel like you hit a dead end or a very high speed bump. Once you're done freaking out, breathe in and out and keep going. There WILL be many challenges ahead, all app developers who had great ideas and great products had their own sets of unique challenges. What separates them from the rest is their ability to overcome these hurdles and to stand by their plans and ideas.

- **Manage your expectations.** Yes, it's every app developers dream to be an overnight millionaire. Unfortunately, less than 5% of ALL app developers see this dream to reality and those that did, didn't expect for their app to make them millionaires. If you set your expectations to a more practical and manageable level, you will be able to adjust your plans and strategies accordingly to fit the situation.

App development is an exciting field to enter because it is dynamic, fast-paced and ever-changing industry. More and more people are reaching for the latest smartphone model and even the newest tablet. This industry is not even at its peak yet and it gives rookie developers like you the opportunity to become a part of it at the most optimum time.

18. Conclusion

Even those with zero app programming skills can get into the business of app development. There have been successful apps created by rookies who had the right idea, the right strategy and the right execution to make themselves overnight millionaires.

Of course, the road isn't easy and there will be a lot of challenges ahead. One of the most difficult and time-consuming tasks in app development is brainstorming the type of app that you want to produce. You will spend a lot of time reflecting and researching during this stage of the process but it will all be worth it.

Great ideas are not rushed or forced. In fact, some of the greatest and most creative app ideas came from unexpected "eureka" moments. Always keep your smartphone handy so that you can immediately begin researching every idea as it comes. Check the app store for similar apps to gauge whether it's an idea worth pursuing.

Competition for app revenues and rankings are getting tougher as the industry gets more crowded with new developers trying to get a piece of thee action. Now is the perfect time for you to establish yourself in the app industry for two main reasons.

First, you can learn from established developers. By studying their experiences and examples, you'll have a good idea of how to go about developing your app. These individuals were the ones who helped shape the app environment of today.

Second, there are now a wide myriad of tools to help you in every aspect of app development. Whether it's a drag-and-drop app builder or websites that connect you with developers-for-hire, everything you need can be available to you if you know where to find them.

App development isn't just a one-step process. Even after you have launched your app, you are still responsible for its success in terms of sales, downloads and reviews. Building rapport with you customers is one of the most effective ways for you to market and promote your app. Not all developers have multi-million dollar marketing budgets and as a rookie developer, your best and most practical marketing technique would be to provide good customer service to match a good product.

Your effort will be your number one investment for app development. Once people see that you care about delivering value added services for your product, they will feel more comfortable listening to your subtle sales pitches. Developing a loyal customer base will also help you in the future should you decide to apply monetization techniques like inapp purchases or upgrades.

You too can become the app developer *du jour* and as you have read in this e-book, it's really not as difficult as a lot of people expect it to be. With careful planning, a lot of brainstorming and a good working relationship with the right people, you too can infiltrate the robust app industry and make a name for yourself.

19. THANK YOU FOR READING!

Thank You so much for reading this book. If this title gave you a ton of value, It would be amazing for you to leave a REVIEW !

THANK YOU FOR DOWNLOADING! IF YOU WOULD LIKE TO BECOME APART OF OUR READER COMMUNITY AND RECEIVE UPDATES ON UPCOMING TITLES PLEASE EMAIL PARAMOUNTPUBLISHINGCO@ GMAIL.COM

Made in the USA
Middletown, DE
16 August 2016